A WORD IN YOUR EAR
HISTORY ABOUT ST. IVES

TOM RICHARDS

historical articles first published in
THE ST. IVES TIMES & ECHO

A Word in Your Ear

© Tom Richards

First edition published 2006

Reproductions appearing in this edition retain all rights still applicable to the original copyright proprietors, who have been credited where their identity is known.

Printed & Published by:
St. Ives Printing & Publishing Company,
High Street, St. Ives, Cornwall TR26 1RS, UK

ISBN 0 948385 41 3

CONTENTS

INTRODUCTION

The articles in this book were not written to a pattern but in several cases followed events or suggestions. The *Trevessa* saga, for instance, resulted from the display of a survivor's log on television in Bristol; the biographical feature on Dr. Bottrell and Paraguay from Mr. Edward Ninnes telling me of the memorial in Barnoon cemetery, while the feature on D.H. Lawrence and the engines off Clodgy Point from a bet in a pub in Plymouth, and a request to the *Times & Echo* for information. In one way or another they reflect aspects of the town's history and it is my hope that they will be of interest not only to those of us of a certain age but also a wider audience.

I was born in No.7 Virgin Street, the house on the right at the top of the steps and not long after we moved to No.26 - The Retreat - at the far end. The fisherman carrying home some wood was Mr. John Stoneman. The lady in the background was Mrs. Thomasina Rowe and the young lady on the left is Mrs. Williams.

FOREWORD

Tom is a brilliant researcher and local historian. Had he lived earlier he would certainly have qualified as an assistant to Sherlock Holmes! He has that special ability to think laterally, together with a wry smile and confidence that comes with his love of his fellow Cornish so that they really want to help him get to the bottom of a good story. That is evident in these articles originally published in *The St. Ives Times & Echo*.

Given any local subject Tom will focus his full attention on it. I recall on one occasion he asked me for the name of the wreck with railway engines on its deck, sunk off Clodgy Point in the 1914-1918 war. "Don't know" said I. Within an hour he came back with the name and its position. A week later I received a card which read: "Have read a translation of the log of the U-boat captain who sank the vessel". Later he had the name of the Scottish company who had made the engines, and the fact that this was the second ship carrying engines from the same makers which had been sunk on its way to France. This type of research happened again and again and I am pleased to see this story in the collection.

Cornishmen are known to be great travellers for work in hard times and many of Tom's generation exported their talent worldwide, rather than follow their forebears into the fishing industry. So Tom spent his working life away from his town of birth, but the ties were always strong and his interest in and love of his hometown and its inhabitants never forgotten. That is why this selection of his articles is so important, as a delightful record of the town's past, and a testament to its future.

D. Harding Laity

31 August 1990

WHAT'S IN IT FOR ME?
St. Ives and the 1881 Census

When I mentioned to a friend that I reckoned it would take me about 40 hours to transcribe a section of the 1881 British Census he asked: 'How much do they pay per hour?' I explained it was voluntary — no pay or expenses. He pondered this for a few moments and then asked: 'Well, what's in it for you then?'. The answer was much the same as would be given by any of the hundreds of volunteers up and down the country — the satisfaction of being able to contribute to a project which will benefit generations to come. If he had asked that question after I had completed my transcription I could have added that there was a lot in it for me in the Census itself.

When Moira Tangye asked for volunteers for the 1881 census project I offered to transcribe part of St. Ives parish. My family have lived in St. Ives for many generations; I was born in Virgin Street and it would be easier for me to decipher the names of streets and residents than if I were to tackle foreign parts such as Redruth or Perranuthnoe. Also I hoped I might find references to my own Richards, Geen and Faull forebears. When my parcel arrived I was delighted that it contained the whole of Downlong St. Ives, (except for Fore Street) from Virgin Street and Market Strand to Wheal Dream and the Island.

Transcription was not difficult provided the conventions were observed, although it was essential to concentrate and not let the mind wander. In a number of cases the enumerator's mind had wandered when he showed the occupation of fishermen's wives as fishermen and transposed the ages of males and females. These, however, were minor details. My enumerator's handwriting was not too bad and I was able to decipher nearly everything except for a few Christian names. Help was however at hand. A relative who is 89 and remembers many of the families was able to tell me the names and family connections of those I could not identify.

The enumerator's sheets themselves are of interest. In many cases houses either had no numbers or the enumerator didn't include them, and locations are related to the occupier. At the beginning of each batch of sheets is a list of the streets which are covered, and include such entries as 'Norway Square to Capt. Thos. Richards' shop, Norway Lane,' and 'Virgin Street (on both sides including courts and alleys) from

Jenkyns house to the Digey Corner.' Some street names have long since disappeared from use — Williams Row for example. Formerly known as George Williams Row it is now Porthmeor Road. Bamfields Row is one I have not yet located. All the familiar names are there — Virgin Street, Love Lane, the Digey, Hicks Court, Teetotal Street, Mount Zion etc. — with one exception. Pudding Bag Lane is gone, demolished in 1936 to make way for the Sloop car park. In some cases the enumerator wrote the names as they sounded. What has long been called 'The Meadow' is shown simply as 'Medow,' while the present Carncrows Street is shown as 'Carncrouse Street.'

It is a rare privilege to have at home even for a short while the census details for a whole community. It was too good an opportunity to miss, and I extracted information which gives snapshots of the social scene Downlong 109 years ago.

There has always been a distinct division between Downlong, basically the harbour area below the Market Place, and Uplong, the area above the Market Place which included the more prosperous families of the town. The two areas even had their own weekly newspaper — *The Western Echo* was the Downlong paper, *The St. Ives Times* for Uplong. Both are now combined in *The St. Ives Times & Echo*. In 1881 the Council housing estates at Ayr, at the top of the town, were still many years away, and the fishermen lived as a close community in the streets and alleyways around and within a few minutes walk of the harbour.

The West Cornwall Railway branch line from St. Erth had been opened four years earlier in 1877, but mass tourism was a long way off, and the town depended on fishing and mining, although as in many other areas of Cornwall, mining was in decline.

The Downlong section of the census covered some 2618 persons, made up of 617 households. The number of males in employment Downlong was some 760 and of these 572 were fishermen, their ages ranging from 14 to 84. I found only one fisherboy, T. Trevorrow, age 15, grandson of Mr. Thomas Roach of Teetotal Street. Fishing provided employment not only for fishermen but also a variety of supporting occupations. Sail lofts were used by the six sailmakers living Downlong for making and mending the sails used by the fleet.

Nets were mended at home and in the net lofts by members of fishing families, and 54 women and girls, known as beadsters, indicated they were employed on this work. Within the next twelve years or so many of these lofts would be empty and silent, while some would be used by artists such as Olsson, Grier and Stokes. Today only one or two remain as working lofts, the rest having been demolished or converted to cafes or holiday apartments. Recently one group of sail lofts in Bethesda Hill, the last of their type in the harbour area, has been converted into a prestigious suite of offices.

Mr. John Craze, rope-maker, lived in the Digey, and Mr. Thomas Hambly, boat builder, lived in Porthmeor Square. Six shipwrights and ships carpenters lived in the streets near the harbour. Baskets were made by four basket-makers and a cooper, Mr. Warren of Teetotal Street provided the barrels, the iron hoops probably being made by one or other of the three blacksmiths. The bulk of the fish was sent away by rail to inland markets and for export, but some was sold locally. Twenty-six people worked as buyers, salesmen and hawkers. The five carriers who lived Downlong no doubt used their horses and carts to convey the barrels from the harbour to the railway station.

Fishermen tended to stick to fishing, although some, like my grandfather, spent summer months abroad as crew members on steam yachts owned by the wealthy. I found only one man described as 'tin miner and fisherman,' Mr. James Roach Major of 42 Virgin Street. Mr. Charles Rowe of 28 Virgin Street, however, is described as 'fisherman and Borough Auditor.'

Miners often left the mines in the summer to go fishing, and only one miner is recorded as living Downlong, another Mr. Major, at 44 Virgin Street. There was also a mine carpenter, Mr. William Thomas, and his son Matthew, a mine blacksmith.

Mr. John French, nephew of Mr. William Rouse of 21 Virgin Street is described as an 'engineer out of employ.' The minutes of the first meeting of the Institution of Civil Engineers in 1818 described an engineer as 'a mediator between the Philosopher and the working mechanic, and like an interpreter between two foreigners must understand the language of both.' Mr. French might well have been an interpreter between the fishermen and the miners as they used different words and expressions, but he was probably a mechanical engineer who had worked on the machinery and pumping engines in one of the local mines which had closed down.

Connections with the sea were not confined to fishermen. The sea captains mostly lived Uplong, but Downlong there were 60 men described as master mariners, mariners or sailors, and there were many mariners' wives who were temporarily heads of household as their husbands were abroad. Sadly there were also mariners' widows. Mr. William Herbert, of Chy-an-Chy, whose sons William and Edward ran the grocer's shop (now the sub-Post Office), is recorded as a Naval and Greenwich Pensioner. Shipping in and out of St. Ives, Lelant and Hayle was extensive. These local movements and the deep sea vessels on passage to ports up channel required the services of the four pilots and three branch pilots who lived Downlong. Safety at sea was assisted by Mr. John Veal of Bethesda Road, who, at the age of 80, was described as 'light keeper,' a task which, I am told, involved attending daily to the light at the end of the breakwater.

Apart from work associated with fishing the most popular occupation for women and girls was that of tailoress, of whom there were 62. There were also 33 dressmakers, 5 drapers and assistants, and 3 milliners. There were 23 general and domestic servants, and one 17-year old was described as a ladies maid, employed probably in one of the big houses Uplong. Mrs. Cocking of 1, Carncrous Street is shown as a 'stay maker.' My relative remembers the stays made by this lady which were sold in Mr. Comley's shop in Fore Street and were made with coarse cloth from soldiers uniforms. As a child she was intrigued by the way they creaked when worn by elderly aunts. Laundrettes had not then been invented. Four women worked as laundresses and three as manglewomen, providing a public mangling service or do-it-yourself. Domestic cleaning was provided by twelve charwomen and three chargirls.

Shops Downlong were generally small grocers and general dealers, sometimes using the front room of a house. The fact that it was a shop would be advertised by placing a packet of tea in the window. There were 33 persons shown as grocers and shopkeepers, many of them widows or the wives of miners or sailors working away from home. In Porthmeor Square, Mr. Peter Veal at the age of 74, is described as 'fisherman and small grocer,' while his daughter Sarah 'attends the shop.' Mr. Matthew Trevorrow, a butcher, lived at Chy-an-Chy, and Mrs. Uren of 8 Mount Zion is described as a tea dealer. Daughter Pauline 1940 or 41 or 42

There were five bakers, including Mr. William Trevorrow, whose bakehouse near the Old Arch in Hicks Court was still in use by his family in my time. I recall many occasions when I would take a joint to the bakehouse, although I wasn't allowed to collect it when cooked. There were five shoemakers and two milk sellers. Mr. John Hollow had his coalyard in the Digey, and Mr. Sam Lawry the hairdresser lived in Fish Street. The Town Crier, Mr. Charles Paynter, lived in St. Peters Street. Mr.

Adam Lander, who lived in Fish Street, is described as auctioneer, but it is not stated whether he auctioned fish, goods and chattels, or houses.

Man cannot live by bread alone, and the thirsty folk of Downlong were catered for by three establishments. Mrs. Elizabeth Richards at the White Hart Inn on the Wharf described herself as Hotel Keeper. Her late husband George had his own brewhouse in Fish Street, which, after his death, was taken over by the Redruth Brewery Co. Mr. George Wasley of the Sloop described himself as Innkeeper. Mrs. Hannah Quick of the Dolphin, Chy-an-Chy, was more down to earth and described herself as Beerhouse Keeper. The Dolphin has gone but the Sloop is still there.

About the end of the first world war the White Hart became Mr. Laity's shop specialising in exotic teas and coffee. I remember the fascination his shop window had for us lads, with its models of Chinese junks, its oriental vases and lanterns and large red coffee grinders, but especially the plates with samples of tea from all over the Far East. We particularly liked the blocks of tea from Mongolia which looked like chewing tobacco. Mongolia was completely beyond our comprehension!

Few tradesmen seemed to live Downlong. I found only eight joiners or carpenters and one mason. The Gas Works Engineer lived in the Company house in the works, and one of his fitters, Mr. James Bosanquet, lived not far away in Porthmeor Square.

Defence of the realm against invasion or pirates was looked after by two soldiers, Gunman William Ahern from Ireland, and Bombardier James Cord from London, who lived with their families in the two houses adjoining the coastal battery at the top of the Island. The three gun battery was dismantled in 1895, no doubt due to defence cuts. The houses continued in occupation for many years but are now let as studios.

At first glance the description Farmer and Gardener applied to Mr. Robert Williams of Fish Street seems out of place, but he probably grazed cows on the Island Meadow slopes, a practice continued within living memory.

While there may have been shortages of money and material possessions there was no shortage of children, of whom 611 were shown as scholars at ages ranging from 2 to 16. The actual number was probably higher as the status of some children of school age was not recorded. In addition there were 221 children recorded as infants or 'at home.' Large families were common, with children arriving at intervals of about two years. Many families were supplemented by aged parents as well as grandchildren, nieces and nephews, particularly if one or other of the childrens' parents had died. Grandparents often helped out by taking children into their homes if there was a problem with accommodation or if times were hard.

Births were at home and this must have involved constant work for doctors and midwives. Doctors and nurses lived Uplong, but one young nurse, Eliza Toman, is shown as living at St. Eia Street. Mrs. Elizabeth Quick is described as Monthly Nurse, whose job it was to live with a family for the first month after the arrival of a baby, to look after them and help the mother after her two weeks in bed. William and John Richards, aged 4 and 2, had been born in Michigan, USA, no doubt in the mining camps of Calumet or the Keweenaw peninsula in Michigan on Lake Superior. Father was possibly still over there, working as a hard-rock miner, as the boys were living at 3 Carn Glaze with their mother Jane who was described as 'miner's wife.' The two daughters of Mr. Richard Quick, fish merchant of 7 Bunkers Hill, were born in Australia.

Island Road school was not yet built, so some scholars would have attended the National (C of E) school, while others the privately run schools in school rooms and houses like that run by Miss Sarah (Sally) Mankey, school mistress, and her sister Elizabeth, school assistant, who lived at No.1 Digey. Others would have been among those who entered the new Board School in the Stennack when it opened its doors in January 1881, three months before the Census. Classes of 40 or 50 were commonplace, but the children learned their basic 3 R's and the multiplication tables. Five teachers lived Downlong, including Bessie Clark of 7 Wharf, described as pupil teacher aged 14.

The community was very self-contained. With few exceptions all were born in St. Ives or adjacent areas such as Halsetown or Zennor. Some fishermen brought back brides from their fishing excursions. Mr. Thomas Bryant's wife, Sarah, was born in Ardglass, Ireland, a regular port of call for St. Ives boats engaged in fishing the Irish grounds, and Mr. Thomas Bassett's wife, Ann, came from Peel, Isle of Man. Margret, the wife of Mr. Richard Perkin, mariner, was born in Queenstown, Ireland, and when she came to live with Richard at 24 Digey, her invalid mother Kate, also from Queenstown, came to live with them. Some St. Ives girls captured husbands from distant parts. Susan Watty of 1 Virgin Street was born in St. Ives, but her husband, William, a ships carpenter, came from Belfast. Other husbands were from Lancashire and Lowestoft.

Very few people suffered from infirmities, one or two being shown as blind or deaf or crippled from birth.

There are still interesting facts and facets of Downlong life which could be extracted from the Census — that will be for another day — but what I have mentioned shows there was a lot in it for me, and as we say in Cornwall, what started out as a labour of love turned out to be a proper job!

And what of my own family connections? My Richards and Faulls lived outside the area covered by my sheets, but I did find my Geens, including my grandmother, Elizabeth Catherine, aged 15. I still have much to do on our connections with Baragwanath, Curnow, Faull, Hodge, Perkin, Trevorrow, etc, but no doubt the census will reveal more interesting information.

Following the publication of this article I was informed by the late Mrs Annie Allen (nee Paynter), whose family owned property in Porthmeor Square, that the basket makers softened the withies for the baskets in a pool in the Square.

DR. JAMES F.H. BOTTRELL MRCSE LSA
The Philanthropical Physician and the St. Ives/Paraguay connections

For centuries the great and the good have been honoured and remembered by having places named after them. Cornwall, Wales and Brittany have a proliferation of places named after Saints and St. Ives has its own St. Ia. The town also has Wesley Place and local people are remembered with such names as Hain Walk, Flamank's Court and Halsetown. Discovering a place, a river or a mountain could almost guarantee having it named after you. Cecil Rhodes had a country named after him and Queen Victoria did very well with a state in Australia, a lake and a waterfall in Africa and an island in Canada.

There are not many places in the world left to be discovered, so names of people are now applied to public buildings, roads in new housing estates or University Halls of Residence, particularly if they come with an endowment. A fairly recent example is the naming of a ward in a major London hospital after St. Ives-born Percy Lane Oliver OBE who developed the system of voluntary blood donors. Most places can be matched with individuals whose names they bear, but I suspect there are few people who are aware of a connection between a man who is buried in Barnoon cemetery in St. Ives and a small town in Paraguay in central South America which is named after him. The man was Dr. James Bottrell MRCSE LSA, and the town is called Colonia Bottrell.

Dr. Bottrell's grave is in the upper section above the chapel on the Clodgy side and the headstone records that he died on June 23rd 1912. At the foot of the grave is a granite block on which is mounted a bronze plaque. The plaque, made by J. Gorruzzo & Co in Buenos Aires, Argentina, measures some 18 by 10 inches. On the left side is depicted a woman in flowing garments, seated and extending her right hand to a woman and child. On the right side of the plaque are the words, in English: *In memoriam. To the Philanthropical Physician Doctor James F.H. Bottrell. His friends from Paraguay 1914.* Over the years the sea air and the salt spray from Porthmeor beach have weathered the plaque to a mellow green, but the detail is as good now as the day it left the Gorruzzo workshops.

So what did Dr. Bottrell do to merit such a splendid memorial, what was the Paraguay connection, and what brought him to St. Ives towards the end of his life? No family connections with St. Ives have yet been discovered, although Bottrell is a respected name in the town and elsewhere in Cornwall, going back to the time of William the Conqueror.

I recall the tall figure of Reggie Bottrell, a railway guard at St. Ives station when I joined the service there in 1940. A more distant Bottrell with St. Ives connections was Catherine or Kitty Bottrell who married a Breton fisherman Jean Lemal in 1709 and lived at Carn Glaze. Jean was drowned in the bay and his widow and eight daughters were known as 'the nine Lemals,' a name given to a local version of marbles. Kitty achieved notoriety with her intervention in the election of 1768 when she poured a stocking full of guineas into the hands of Dr. John Stevens of Trowan, the popular candidate, unfortunately to no avail. Dr. Stevens went to live in France and had no more success there with a Lottery ticket which he bought for his brothers at Trowan. It drew a blank.

At the outset of the investigation into the background to Dr. Bottrell I thought there must be someone in the town connected with him as his grave was well cared for, with daffodil bulbs planted in the earth. A message left on the grave in a jam jar produced a response from Mrs. Eleanora Elliott (née Miners) of Richmond Place who confirmed she has no Bottrell connections, but when visiting her family grave nearby she regularly tidied Dr. Bottrell's grave and it was she who planted the bulbs. Mrs. Elliott also was intrigued by the plaque and felt it was not much to do for someone who evidently had done good to his fellow men.

James Francis Henry Bottrell was born at The Friars, St. Nicholas, Hereford on 30th April 1855, the son of William Bottrell, auctioneer and Sheriff's Officer for the County of Hereford and his wife Harriet. In the 1871 census the family also included two elder daughters, an 11-year old grand-daughter, a housemaid, a cook and a groom. In 1877 James gained his Membership Diploma (MRCSE) of the Royal College of Surgeons of England and the LSA (Licentiate of the Society of Apothecaries), both of which were necessary to become a general practitioner.

The term 'Apothecary' originally described someone who dispensed medicines and who these days would be called a pharmacist. His first listing in the Medical Register showed him in practice at Hereford in 1878 and again in 1879. In 1880 he moved to the Hospital for Women in Soho Square, London, as Resident Physician, and at some time between then and 1889 he was a Surgeon with the Royal West India Mail Service whose ships served the islands of the Caribbean.

His name does not appear in the Medical Register for the years 1890 to 1895 – he may have gone abroad and not notified his whereabouts — but from 1896 to 1912 he is shown as living at Villaricca, Paraguay, South America. It is not clear when or why he went to Paraguay but he clearly intended to stay as his wife and small children accompanied him. He may have gone following an appeal from the Government of the day as two other British doctors went as well. Paraguay was a country left devastated after a six-year war (1864-1870) against the Triple Alliance of Argentina, Uruguay and Brazil. For many years in the aftermath of the war there was much hunger and illness, with a dearth of professional and medical services. It seems likely that the Paraguay authorities would have sought help from overseas and that Bottrell with his specialist knowledge of tuberculosis and associated ailments responded to the call. Apart from the possibility of appeals from the Paraguay authorities it could be that in the course of his voyages to the Caribbean as Ship's Surgeon he would have heard of the conditions there and the desperate need for medical expertise.

His two companions must have found the conditions in Paraguay were more than they had bargained for as they soon returned to Britain. Bottrell, however, settled in Villaricca, a town south-east of the capital Asunción, where he had a two-storey house built and in which he conducted a clinic as a Tisiologist, 'a doctor of consumption.' The house is still there, no longer in the ownership of Bottrell's descendants, but his memory is kept alive by one of the main streets named 'Calle Doctor Bottrell' – with the accent on the final syllables.

His speciality was the treatment of tuberculosis and it would appear that he settled in Villaricca as the location was deemed to have an ideal climate for those with lung problems, with 'open-air' treatment which may have been similar to that at the sanatorium at Tehidy. This did not work for my mother but appears to have been very successful for Dr. Bottrell's patients. The demand for his services outstripped the capability of the clinic in his residence so he set up a new clinic on a piece of land he owned near Villaricca. His reputation as a caring physician must have been widely-known and highly respected as patients came from as far afield as Argentina to seek his help. Around the clinic grew a community which was named after him — Colonia Bottrell.

Present-day Colonia Bottrell is a town of some 1,700 inhabitants. At the crossroads in the town centre the Government have built a new Health Centre (Centro de Salud) named 'Ministry of Public Health. Dr. Bottrell Health Centre.' The Centre has beds for a small number of patients and is staffed by two nurses. They still do sputum tests and a small laboratory has been set up for other types of analysis including AIDS tests. Adjoining the Centre is the town police station — one room with one resident officer and over the door the imposing signs 'Judicial Power of the Republic of Paraguay' and 'Justice of the Peace of Bottrell.' Transport is mostly pick-up trucks with the number plates carrying the vehicle number plus 'Dr. Bottrell Paraguay.' Notices are in Spanish, the official language, but many residents speak almost exclusively Guarani, Paraguay's native language.

These days one can imagine Dr. Bottrell working for one of the overseas aid agencies with all the back-up and resources of international organisations. He probably had very limited facilities and basic equipment, and it was the use of basic equipment which led to his untimely death.

One night, in the town of Coronel Oviedo, he was operating on a patient who had been carried on an ox-cart from a town in north-eastern Paraguay and who had a serious infection of his jaw resulting from a bullet wound. The operation was being carried out by the light of a hurricane lamp held by a nurse. The nature of the operation so upset the nurse that she fainted and dropped the lamp which went out. In the darkness Dr. Bottrell accidentally cut himself with his scalpel, the wound turned septic and he was forced to his bed. Eventually it was decided he should go to England, but it is not clear whether this was in the hope of treatment or an acceptance that he had only a limited period left to live and that he would spend his remaining days in his native land.

One of his last acts before leaving Paraguay was to donate part of his lands, divided by him into plots, to an institution which gave credit to farmers and people buying land, to be sold on credit to the families already resident on his land, most of whom had lived there from the creation of the community.

It is not known when he returned to England or why he and his family chose to come to St. Ives. There was a West Country connection as while his father was born in Leominster his mother was born in Plymouth. In the 1871 Census his father was aged 77, while his mother was 38 and one can speculate that when his father died the family may have moved to the South-West.

We also do not know how long they were in St. Ives before Dr. Bottrell died at Eden House on 23rd June 1912. Eden House had been bought by the Pearce family from the executors of the Treweeke estate in 1909, but as they did not occupy it until several years later it would have been rented by Dr. Bottrell. The report of his death in the *Western Echo* referred to '. . . a comparatively short residence in the town during which time he had made many friends . . .' and that he had been suffering 'from a painful malady.' *The St. Ives Times* report said that he had been residing in the town for some time '. . . for the benefit of his health . . .' and that he had received much care and attention.

Among the floral tributes were several from friends in Paraguay, and the plaque which they commissioned in Buenos Aires and which is on the grave in Barnoon testifies to the esteem in which he was held and the sincerity of their regard for him. There is also an intriguing reference in the newspaper report to a floral tribute 'from the two maids to dear master.' They are not named but the death was registered by Jane T. Humphreys who was present at the death. The 1891 census records a Jane Humphreys aged 10, the daughter of Richard and Jane Humphreys, living in the Digey, and, at 31 she may have been one of the maids.

One of Dr. Bottrell's sons in Paraguay fought in world war one in Europe and returned to settle in Villaricca. Other children went to Africa and England. A grandson, Señor Peter Bottrell, is a rancher at Coronel Oviedo, ironically the part of the country where his grandfather met what was to be the cause of his death, and he has many souvenirs of him, including beautiful ponchos given to him by grateful patients. Dr. Bottrell's death at 57 robbed the people of Paraguay of a dedicated medical man and one wonders what other good work he would have done if the nurse had not dropped the hurricane lamp.

On occasions when I visit the graves of my family in Barnoon I find myself acting as unofficial guide to wandering Tate Gallery visitors looking for the grave of Alfred Wallis — (the Tate Management may like to consider producing a small leaflet with directions). For many their main interest is not so much the man as the Bernard Leach tiles which cover him and it pleases me to take the opportunity of showing them the plaque on Dr. Bottrell's grave and telling them of the man who worked among the people of Paraguay, who lost his life in the course of his humanitarian efforts, is honoured in a foreign land and fully justified the appellation of 'The Philanthropical Physician.'

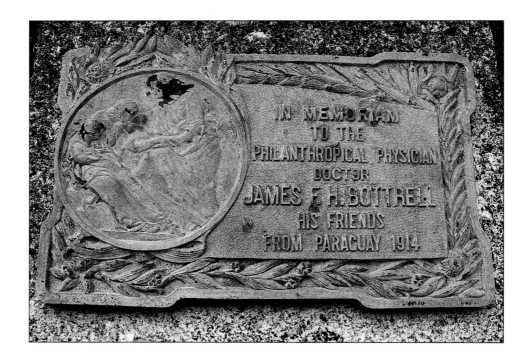

THE FISHERMEN'S CO-OP
A St. Ives institution

Since 1920 many things have changed in St. Ives, not least the shops and business establishments which serviced the local community. At that time and for many years after, it was possible to buy almost anything in St. Ives, with an abundance of shops including a wide choice of general dealers, grocers, drapers, butchers, outfitters etc. Today many of those businesses of yesteryear are only a memory and the shops they occupied are now geared towards the tourist trade. One establishment, however, has survived — the Fishermen's Co-op, or to give it the correct title The United Fishermen's Co-operative Society (St. Ives) Ltd, which continues to trade, albeit in a different market.

In its early days the shop on the Wharf was the place where boys would go to buy mulley hooks and skiliven for their Saturday morning activities and their elders would go to buy the commodities needed to service the fishing fleet. It was familiar to everyone Downlong and was no ordinary shop. I recall it in the 1930's as an Aladdin's cave, crowded with all manner of interesting things on the counter, the shelves, the floor and suspended from the beams. Oilskins, leather seaboots, lanterns, glass floats, ropes, nets, nails and screws all jostled for space, and over all was the distinctive but not unpleasant smell of a hardware shop mixed with paraffin and linseed oil.

It is still in its original location on the Wharf, although with changing times the merchandise has changed. It is still the trading base of an organisation which is managed by its members, catering originally for the needs of the fishing industry, but in later years adapting to its decline and the expansion of tourism.

The seeds from which the St. Ives Co-op grew were sown in the House of Commons on the afternoon of 22nd July 1914, when a deputation of seven influential businessmen led by Cecil Harmsworth MP met Mr. Walter Runciman, President of the Board of Agriculture, who later became Viscount Runciman, Member of Parliament for St. Ives between 1929 and 1937. Mr. Runciman had agreed to meet the deputation to hear their representations for Government support for the establishment of an organisation which would serve the interests of inshore fishermen in England and Wales, and encourage co-operative action for the conservation and development of fisheries. The proposals were supported and within a short time the Fisheries Organisation Society Ltd (FOS for short) was set up.

The main objective of FOS was the propagation of co-operative principles among fisheries and allied industries. This included the aim of establishing a Fishermen's Co-operative Society in every inshore fishing port in England and Wales where co-operative trading was desirable and possible. FOS also acted as a focus for protecting the interests of the fishing industry nationally and internationally. Through subsidiary organisations the Society offered comprehensive insurance covering fishing vessels against total loss, damage etc, as well as helping fishermen to buy their boats with reasonably priced loans.

In 1920 it was proposed through FOS that a Fishermen's Co-operative Society should be set up in St. Ives and Mr. William Lawry was asked if he would take on the task of organising it. A local man who had held many civic offices in the town, Mr. Lawry had served in a voluntary capacity as Port Fishery Officer at St. Ives in the first world war, a service for which he was awarded an MBE. He was well known throughout the fishing industry in Cornwall; he was trusted and his commitment to the fishing community made him an obvious choice to steer the new Society to success. Mr. Lawry was involved with FOS from the earliest days.

He served as Secretary and Treasurer of its subsidiary the Cornish Fishing Vessels Insurance Society Ltd from its foundation until he was 80 years of age, helping many Cornish fishermen to purchase their vessels and safeguard their investment. Mr. Lawry's work on behalf of FOS and the fishing industry was recognised in 1962 when he accepted an invitation to become a Vice-President of the Society.

On the 14th January 1920 a meeting of about 70 interested fishermen was held in the Town Hall at which it was unanimously agreed that a St. Ives Society should be formed for trading purposes only. Some Societies, particularly at ports in Lancashire and on the East coast handled the marketing of members' catches as well as trading in goods. Others were formed for the provision of equipment such as the Co-operative Winch Societies at Gorran Haven and Mullion Cove. A Society at Conway was set up for the specific purpose of acquiring and operating an ice plant for the benefit of the local fleet. Each Society decided its own name. These ranged from the Aldeburgh Fishermen's Trade Guild Ltd to the Severn Estuary (Nets and Fixed Engines) Fishermen's Association, and it says something for St. Ives that it was the only Society in England and Wales to have the word 'United' in its title.

A Committee was set up and the following day a sub-committee met to receive share capital in a fishing loft on Mount Zion. Prospective members were asked £1 for a share, but some had sufficient faith to put in £75 and £100. My grandfather bought share No. 52 which passed to my father and has now passed to me. I hope it will stay in the family.

A Secretary/Manager was appointed, premises for use as a shop were rented on the Wharf, and the first order was for 10 pilchard nets and two mackerel nets with a request to the supplier for longer credit. It is not recorded whether they received a favourable response.

The next order was for ½ ton of carbide, 12 oilskin frocks, 12 barwells, 12 souwesters, 2 dozen tar brushes, paint brushes and one cwt of white paint, the carbide being required for the vessels lanterns.

Business was evidently expanding as in October 1920, when a bark house and yard near the Island, offered for sale under their own control, represented an important part of the co-operative nature of the enterprise, and the following rules were drawn up to regulate the use of the facility:

1. To be at the disposal of every person who wishes to bark.

2. That the first boat ready to bark be allowed to do so if the person in turn cannot take it in a reasonable time.

3. That the boiler furnace be lit for two boats as a minimum, but if the person who wishes to bark is prepared to bear the extra expense the boiler be lit.

Bark house bills were sent out at the end of every season, the charges being set at 5/- for a tackle and lance net, 5d per net herring and pilchard, and 2d per net, mackerel. For curing the charge was 5s.0d for small furnace.

By the late 1970's the bark house was little used, so the steam boiler was sold for scrap and the property turned into lofts. It is believed it was the last bark house to be used as such in the country, and the last boats to use it were from Newlyn and Mevagissey.

A major decision in October 1920 was to increase the membership by accepting fishermen from other towns as share-holders. This meant that boats from Newlyn or elsewhere could purchase their requirements at St. Ives and share in the financial benefits. The Society now included coal in their list of sales and in November 1920 a truck was ordered from the factors for delivery to St. Ives station and from there to the old lifeboat house which adjoined the bark house and served as a store, and subsequently a lorry was purchased for haulage. On Christmas Eve the Committee agreed to order ½ ton of Burmah cutch, the material used in the barking process. Presumably the members chose to hold their meeting on Christmas Eve to keep out of the way of the household activities.

By March 1921 the business was well established and it was agreed at a meeting on the 14th March to pay shareholders a dividend of 5% on share capital. A year later shareholders had a bonus as in addition to receiving 5% on capital they were also offered a dividend of 2½% on purchases. This latter payment represented a considerable attraction and an added inducement to buy a wide range of domestic necessities through the Society.

A major event in the history of the Society occurred in April 1922 when the rented property on the Wharf was purchased. The purchase included a number of cottages, part of which had formerly been the Ship Aground Inn. The year 1922 was not a good one so far as the fishing community were concerned. The *Western Echo* reported in January 1923 that the herring season had been disastrous for the majority of men, not only because of the scarcity of fish but also the loss of and damage to nets due to the depredations of dogfish. As a result many fishermen appeared before the Bench to explain why they had defaulted on the payment of their rates. Even though this affected the business of the Co-op the Committee were mindful of the needs of others and in March authority was given to distribute out of the funds, seven pairs of boots to deserving cases as per necessity, and as a goodwill gesture at Christmas coal was sent to the Fishermens Lodges.

The 1923/24 season improved to the extent that in January a steamer loaded a cargo of herrings for Glasgow, destined for the USA, having been cured in the Western Cellars near the Island, and in February 1925 the *Western Echo* reported that over 600 men were employed in the herring fisheries. Business in the Co-op was increasing and in March 1925 an Assistant Secretary was appointed and a year later, with an eye to the future, the Committee agreed to take on a boy apprentice who could be trained in the business.

In 1927, to improve the Society's financial position, the houses which formed part of the property on the Wharf were sold, with purchasers having first refusal of the underneath parts if and when the shop came up for sale. One house over the shop was retained as a store and now provides income for the Society as holiday accommodation.

In 1931 it was decided that employees should cease to be employed at 70 years of age. As a result Mr. Lawry, who had acted as Treasurer from inception, relinquished his position but continued as financial adviser, and the young man who had been taken on as an apprentice was appointed Treasurer in his place, becoming Secretary/Manager four years later.

In 1936 an approach was made to the Post Master asking him to consider the Society becoming a Sub-Post Office, but nothing came of it. Also in 1936 the Spanish Civil War was having an effect on the fishing industry. It was reported that '. . .owing to the trouble in Spain corkwood was advancing in price and it was decided to order next summer's stock immediately. . .' These were not corks for bottles but for nets and floats.

The first effect of the second world war was the loss of Mr. Matthews who was called up in October 1939, Mr. E. Woolcock taking over his duties until his return. Despite shortages and the difficulties of getting merchandise, the Society continued trading and in January 1940 H. Ward was taken on as an errand boy at 10s.0d.

a week. He did the job for twelve months and when he handed in his notice in December J. Polmear was appointed in his place. In the meantime Mr. E. Stratton had been appointed to drive the lorry. A further blow occurred in June 1941 when Anthony Rowe, the Secretary, was called up. Mr. S. Cocking was appointed to take over, with Mrs. Uren (Norah Beckerleg) assisting as lady clerk. A year later Mr. Cocking was in hospital, leaving Mrs. Uren and Mr. Lawry to carry on the business, and in January 1943 Mr. R. Kerfoot was appointed as clerk to assist.

In May 1946 special meetings were convened to discuss the future organisation of the Society as Mr. Lawry, then aged 66, had indicated that he wished to relinquish his responsibilities to the Society without severing his connection. His past services were acknowledged and Mr. G. Cocking was appointed as Secretary. At the same time the share capital dividend was reduced from 5% to 3% and it was also agreed to sell the lorry and advertise the old lifeboat house to let among members. Mr. Sam England bought the lorry for £29.10s.0d., the upper floor of the lifeboat house was let to Mr. W. Barber and the ground floor to Mr. B.G. Stevens.

In April 1947 the share capital dividend was further reduced to 2½%, with a dividend of 3s.0d. in the pound paid on purchases. In the same month Capt. Treloar was appointed Secretary to replace Mr. Cocking. A year later it was decided to discontinue selling coal after 28 years and the coal yard was closed for the sale of coal as from the 30th April 1948.

To rationalise the management of the business Capt. Treloar was appointed Secretary/Manager in December 1952 at a salary of £8 per week, increased to £14 per week in November 1956. The following year the share dividend was back up to 5% with the dividend on purchases increased from 3s.0d. to 4s.0d. in the pound. In November 1958 Capt. Treloar suffered a stroke and the management of the business was taken over on a temporary basis by Mr. Lawry, who was then 78 and his daughter Kitty. Five months later when it was clear that Capt. Treloar would be unable to return to his duties Miss Lawry was appointed Assistant Secretary and at the beginning of 1960 was confirmed as Secretary and provided with a typewriter. She was now a woman manager taking on a job which for the past 40 years had been done by men, and running a business which had changed dramatically over that period.

When the Society started up in 1920 there were some 140 fishing boats registered in St. Ives and the harbour was used by boats from many other Cornish ports as well as by French crabbers from ports in Brittany. By the late 1970's there were only 20 boats engaged in fishing for crayfish, lobsters, crabs, ray, monkfish and turbot, some of them newly-built for this work. These boats used nets and ropes of synthetic materials, supplied by the Co-op. There were also some 60 small boats fishing for mackerel, some part-time but mostly full-time. Leather seaboots were museum pieces, being replaced by lighter weight rubber boots. Floats made of cork were replaced by glass and plastic. Linseed oil was no longer needed for barwells, and cotton nets had given way to nylon which required no barking, hence no cutch, and sails were replaced by engines. Another factor which affected the Society's business was that many fishermen and their families had moved out of the streets Downlong to the Council estates at Ayr, so that household items, paint etc previously bought in the Co-op were more conveniently bought in shops up the street rather than down on the Wharf.

Miss Lawry saw tourism as a business opportunity and as an innovation alongside the washing powder, baking tins and frying pans introduced fashion garments, rubber bathing rings and coloured glass floats which would support no nets in the Bay but were more likely to decorate the kitchens of up-country cottages. One of Miss Lawry's first ventures into the fashion trade was the sale of Cornish fishing smocks, starting with navy blue which was the traditional colour. They were made in Newlyn and as they were essentially working garments, the idea of selling them to tourists was viewed with scepticism by the manufacturers, but the first consignment was an immediate sell-out and they continued as a good line, copied by other retailers and advertised in Sunday newspapers.

They were sold to customers all over the world and someone must have taken some to America as Miss Lawry had a telephone call from a U.S. hospital asking for three dozen to be sent out for nurses who were flying to Vietnam. They were despatched the same day with the appropriate bill and payment was received soon after. On another occasion Madame Tussaud's ordered one for the effigy of Sir Francis Chichester. A photograph of the effigy wearing the Co-op smock was received from Madame Tussaud's but its present whereabouts are unknown. Because of its fine position and interesting contents the shop was frequently used by film location managers, and Miss Lawry recalls return visits by stars to renew acquaintance. She also recalls the old seat reputed to be from the Ship Aground Inn, which was situated outside and was a favourite place for elder members of the fishing fraternity to sit and smoke and recall earlier days.

The year 1963 was a particularly good year for business as indicated in the statistics in the annual report of FOS. Of the 39 Trading Societies in England and Wales St. Ives had the highest membership — 600 — the next being Southend with 149. The St. Ives sales for goods amounted to £31,583, the next being Brixham with 96 members and sales of £4,488. The year was also a sad one for the Society and the town as Mr. Lawry died in April. Many tributes were paid to his life and work, none more fitting than the following from the FOS annual report:

The Society is now one of the leading businesses in St. Ives, and for some years has been the largest Society, both in membership and sales, of the Fishermen's Societies affiliated to the F.O.S. which trade in fishing gear, and there is no question but that its success has been very largely due to the devoted service rendered by Mr. Lawry to the Society as President since its inception. By his passing not only the Society at St. Ives, but the inshore fishing communities in Cornwall will be all the poorer. In 1961, in recognition of his long and honourable record of service to the inshore fishermen of Cornwall, he was made a Vice-President of the FOS.

Miss Lawry resigned as Secretary in 1970 but for a while helped part-time in the shop. Mr. Howard Kernick was appointed as her replacement and under his management the business continued to flourish. On his retirement he also worked part-time in the shop for a while. Mr. Andrew Care, the present Secretary/Manager started work as an assistant in the shop in May 1969 and in December 1974 took over from Mr. Kernick. Andrew is the great-grandson of Mr. Matthew Care who was cashier and shop worker about the late 1940's. The shop as it exists today has changed from what it was in earlier days. In 1989 alterations were made to the internal layout and girders installed to support the premises above.

The Annual General Meeting of the Society is held in December each year and until 1991 these meetings were attended by an officer of the Fishermen's Organisation Society. From the outset FOS took an active interest in the member Societies and one officer in particular, Mr. Lord, regularly attended the meetings at St. Ives over many years. He did much to encourage and support the Society and he was respected and welcomed on his visits to the town. With the passage of time many of the functions of FOS were overtaken by various agencies including the South Western Fish Producer Organisation Limited, which works hard on behalf of West Country fishermen, and FOS was wound up in 1991.

It has already been mentioned that the St. Ives Society was the only one in England and Wales to have 'United' in its title. It also has the distinction of having been managed throughout its 77 years existence by Committees consisting of St. Ives fishermen or their descendants. Former fisherman and Harbour Master, Mr. Gordon Stevens, President of the Society, is probably the longest serving officer after Mr. Lawry. He has been President for over 30 years and is also Chairman of the Committee.

The present Committee members are Mr. E. Bassett, Mr. S. Bassett, Mr. T. Cocking Jnr., Mr. D. Paynter, Mr. J.F. Perkin, Mr. J.M. Perkin, Mr. W.C. Stevens, Mr. M.S. Thomas and Mr. T. Ranson. The work in the barkhouse and the coal store was undertaken by Mr. John Tregurtha, Mr. Philip Paynter and Mr. John Polmear, and among those who have worked in the shop were Mrs. Brown, Mr. Richard Major, Mr. Ian Paynter, Mrs. Carol Rosewarne, Mr. Job Stevens, Mrs. S. Stevens, Mrs. J. Thirlby and Mrs. G. Veal. A member of the staff who was a character in his own right was Mr. William John Stevens. Assisting Mr. Care at the present time are Mrs. P. Jackson and Mrs. J. Perkin.

Many things have changed since 1920. No longer on a winter's evening can you see the Bay filled with the bobbing lights of carbide lanterns, or in the summer months crowded with a hundred or more colourful French crabbers sheltering from approaching bad weather. Apart from going to Camaret the only time you are likely to see a crabber these days is when one comes over from Douarnenez or Audierne to take part in a Festival of the Sea. Even then it will be unlikely that you will hear the click of wooden sabots on the Wharf cobbles or venture to ask the crew Eddie Murt's question 'Plenty long-goose, Johnnie?' and get the reply 'No plenty'. On the other hand, while we no longer hear the accents of Arbroath or Peterhead from kipper girls who came south for a few weeks work in the winter we are pleased to hear accents from all over Scotland as we welcome visitors throughout the year.

The fishing industry in St. Ives as experienced by my grandfather and the other founding members has gone for ever, and the men who bought their Co-op shares on Mount Zion could never have imagined that the time would come when fishermen would be paid to burn or cut up their boats and that parts of their catch would have to be thrown back in the sea to suit the paperwork of bureaucrats in distant offices. It is to be hoped however that for generations to come the shop on the Wharf will continue to display the fascia board of *The United Fishermen's Co-operative Society (St. Ives) Ltd,* and that on 14th January 2020 the flags of all nations will proudly fly from the Lodges to celebrate the centenary and the continued existence of the Fishermen's Co-op — a St. Ives institution.

Incidentally, you can still buy mulley hooks there, although sadly there is not much demand these days from youngsters who look for more sophisticated things to do on Saturday mornings. The shop still offers household goods and if you need paraffin for your emergency lamps or your Primus stove you can buy it there in gallons as well as new-fangled litres. At least some things don't change.

With the passage of time paraffin is no longer sold in the shop!

GREVILLE EWING MATHESON,
his books and Boskerris Vean

Francis Bacon in his essay *Of Studies* said: 'Some books are to be tasted, others to be swallowed, and some few to be chewed and digested'. One thing he didn't mention is that books have to be stored on shelves. Shelf space in Libraries and Record Offices is always a problem, there is never enough, and as the new British Library shows it can be expensive. At home book shelves have to compete for space with the TV, the video, the CD player, the computer, the printer, family photographs and mementoes of foreign holidays. This competition no doubt accounts for the constant supply of books to Charity Shops. Shakespeare tells us that although Prospero apparently had only one book he intended solving his shelf problem by drowning it, while Rosalind had no problem as her books were in the running brooks.

Public Libraries are designed and built for the specific purpose of accommodating large quantities of books but books do not figure in the design of private houses, although some do incorporate a 'study'. In 1920, however, Edmund Fuller in St. Ives was asked by his friend Greville Ewing Matheson to design and supervise the building of a library at Matheson's home in Carbis Bay to accommodate his personal collection of 10,000 books and it is said that he built the library around the bookcases. So how did a collection of this size come to be in Carbis Bay and what do we know of the man who owned it?

Greville Ewing Matheson was born on December 28th 1859 at Soham, Cambridgeshire, into a family with many talents, well-known and respected in their time in literary, academic and political circles. Matheson's grandfather, the Rev. Greville Ewing L.L.D., of Glasgow, his father and uncles were products of the excellent Scottish education system which in their case produced generations of the three D's — Doctors, Dentists and Divines, his father choosing the latter. A hint of Matheson's own future potential is contained in the following letter written to his mother from Soham. He was six years old and it seems that at the time he was staying with relatives:

My dear Mama, I wrote you at London only it was not posted somehow. I need not tell you I like staying here. Tomorrow we are going to play a match against the Stretham. We have got all the hay up. We did not have tea in the hayfield, I do not know why. Uncle Harry has come over today. I have caught four fish with a bowl and stick. I stir the weeds where they live and if they come catch them with the bowl. They are gudgeons. I have a large pan and have put nice clean stones and weeds at the bottom and feed them with these. I am glad that you have been rather busy lately. If I do bath (sic) I shall either go with Herbert or Uncle Frank. I cannot write much more for I want to write a piece of poetry. I am going to have a pair of cricket trowsers, perhaps they will cost 5/-. I have got 4/5½. I can get the rest of the money I think. I must now close my letter. I remain your affeccionate (sic) son Greville Ewing Matheson.

In his future writings he rarely used his own name, but a pen-name, an anagram — M.A. Honest — E.G.Honest MA, or occasionally simply M.A.H., a practice he continued when writing pieces for the *St. Ives Times*.

Matheson was educated at Tettenhall College, Staffordshire and privately, and went to London with his mother's blessing to be among writers and poets. Two of his uncles who were in business in the City lived in Hampstead and it was at their home that he met eminent writers, academics and politicians who were friends of the family. From 1899 to 1907 he edited *The Hampstead Annual,* a literary publication, and was in touch with many of the well-known writers who contributed to its pages.

In the early days in Hampstead Matheson and others in his circle met regularly at Cedar Lawn, the house of a friend, where with tennis and convivial conversation they called themselves the Cedar Lawn Club. Some went overseas to the colonies, others to high office in Church and State, and as a Christmas gift in 1891 Matheson produced for them a book of verses with letters to some eminent members of the Club recalling the happy hours they spent together. He reminded one of them of '. . .days upon the river at Cookham . . . when we ran short of cash, and were saved by your dirty ugly old Balliol blazer, and a cheque drawn out upon a sheet of notepaper. . .'. He published the book for private circulation anonymously but his nom-de-plume fooled none of his friends and their letters in response are tipped in to his copy of the book, making interesting reading in themselves. Later the family moved from Hampstead to Harrow on the Hill.

During his life Matheson met hundreds of interesting people and one of the first was when he was about nineteen. He had written the words of a Fairy Cantata, which was set to music and performed in the school-room attached to the chapel at Oswestry, Shropshire, of which his uncle, the Rev. James Matheson was pastor for some years. There were three mortal children in the cantata, one of whom was acted and sung by a small boy of about ten years of age — Walford Davis. Many years later, when Matheson was living at Carbis Bay, Sir Walford Davis and his wife who were staying in St. Ives, visited for tea and Matheson showed them a copy of the words of the cantata, the music having long since disappeared. When they met again a few days later Sir Walford remembered some of the tunes.

One of the family friends whom he met in Hampstead was Augustine Birrell who was instrumental in influencing Matheson's future. Birrell, the son of a Baptist minister, became a barrister at the age of 25, then an M.P., President of the Board of Education, and Chief Secretary for Ireland, a post from which he resigned following the Easter Rising of 1916. He was well known for his essays and biographies. Matheson was 24 when Birrell introduced him to his brother-in-law who was a son-in-law of Sir Donald Currie and a partner in his firm Donald Currie & Co. whose 'Castle' steamships operated passenger services between Britain and South Africa. As a result of the introduction Matheson joined the firm and became its publicity manager, an occupation to which his talents and personality were admirably suited.

At that time there was fierce competition for the South Africa business between the Castle Line and the Union Line. Currie was a forceful character who began to exploit the value of advertising and publicity and to keep his ships in the news he offered free cruises to notable individuals which Matheson organised and accompanied. Matheson had a fund of stories about these publicity cruises. He recalled one in 1895 which included Mr. and Mrs. Gladstone among a large party of distinguished guests on a twelve day cruise to the opening of the Kiel Canal. Matheson and a friend were on deck when Mr. and Mrs. Gladstone came up and sat down behind them. They heard Mrs. Gladstone say: "Well my dear, I think after that large lunch you ought to walk up and down the deck for a bit." "Large lunch, Catherine?" exclaimed her husband, "What do you mean? I had some soup, a mutton cutlet and a little galantine, do you call that a large lunch?" "Oh well," said Mrs. Gladstone "I'm very glad." "Don't be glad, Catherine, be accurate," thundered Mr. Gladstone.

On another occasion he arranged a lunch for a party of pressmen on one of the Castle line steamers at Blackwall to which the famous conjurer Bertram, a friend and fellow member of the Savage Club, was invited. After lunch Bertram entertained the guests with some of his tricks which included the three thimble trick. This ended with putting a pellet under each thimble. When the thimbles were lifted the pellets had been replaced by small potatoes. When leaving the ship Bertram did his bits and pieces up in a brown paper parcel and on arriving at the gate the policeman in charge asked what was in it. "Oh" said Bertram, "only potatoes, Constable." "Potatoes, Sir?" exclaimed the policeman looking very astonished — "Yes" said Bertram "and excuse me, will you?" and he produced a potato out of the policeman's beard, one out of his helmet, and one out of his coat collar. The policeman looked flabbergasted. "Oh, all right Sir," he stammered and they went on their way.

Matheson had close connections with the press in South Africa and in 1894 was a leading light with several editors of London based South African newspapers in starting The Anglo-African Writers' Club, intended to bring together writers of any description who dealt with South African subjects. He was Hon. Secretary and Rider Haggard was the Chairman. Based in London they were a dining club, with dinners once a month at the Grand Hotel and a guest of the evening. Among those who were entertained were Rudyard Kipling, Sir Arthur Conan Doyle, Sir Donald Currie and numerous M.P.'s. Joseph Chamberlain and Winston Churchill expressed regret that due to pressure of work they were unable to accept invitations, and although Rider Haggard tried to get Cecil Rhodes as a guest when he was in London in 1898 Rhodes declined the invitation. The Club came to an end in 1903, but there is a reminder of Matheson's South Africa connections in a book of his verses *From Veldt and 'Street'; Rhymes more or less South African*, linking the feelings of the exile with the Share Market and the slump on the Stock Exchange. This was published in 1899 under the name M.E. Greville and was very well received by the press in both countries.

In 1900 the Union Line and the Castle Line amalgamated to form the Union Castle Line with Matheson as its publicity manager, a post which he held until his retirement in 1920. He took with him his love of books and created libraries in the Company's ships, an amenity which is standard these days for passengers on cruise ships. Another innovation was the chartering of ships by travel agents. In 1909 Sir Henry Lunn, a friend and neighbour at Harrow, chartered the R.M.S. *Dunottar Castle* and Matheson was sent on her first voyage as representing the Company. This was a Mediterranean cruise lasting more than a month and was before cruising holidays became popular.

Among his many responsibilities was the establishment and development of agencies for booking passages on the Company's ships. In the early 1900's Mr. Ashton who had his chemist's shop and photographic dark room in Market Place, was the Agent in St. Ives for Union Castle services to Africa as well as other shipping lines to Australia, Canada and North and South America. He advertised his Agencies in the *St. Ives Times*. By the time Matheson retired these Agencies had been taken over by Simpson's in Fore Street who continued their *St. Ives Times* advertising.

In 1932 he wrote a series of articles under the title: *Reminiscences of a Publicity Man* which ran for eighteen weeks in *The Newspaper World*. It is hoped that investigation of these and some of the 30 archive boxes of Union Castle Line records held at the National Maritime Museum will provide material for a more comprehensive account of Matheson's work as publicity manager of a passenger shipping line before air travel took over the long hauls and passenger liners became floating hotels for leisurely holiday cruises.

It was through his visits to Cornwall on business that Matheson and his wife Emily grew to love St. Ives and decided that they would make their home there when he retired. They actually settled on Carbis Bay, and a house in Trencrom Lane owned by Squire Tyringham of Trevethoe attracted them. They bought it, had the library built, and moved there in 1920, the start of a happy and fruitful connection with the communities of Carbis Bay and St. Ives. The library extension incorporated what we would now call a 'granny-flat' for Matheson's brother-in-law, Charles John Pugh, a regular contributor to *The St. Ives Times* under the pen-name C.J. Carbis.

Photographs of the completed library show a beautiful room lined with book cases filled with the 10,000 books, many in sets, others in Matheson's own choice of bindings. With a snooker table and comfortable wingchairs it looked an ideal place for winter evenings while the gales roared in from the north-west. Having designed the library Edmund Fuller used it as an Ex Libris bookplate for Matheson, showing him at ease with a cigar and a book, with the French windows open and surrounded by books, his golf clubs and his cricket gear.

The house was named Boskerris after a hamlet in the area. In his *History of St. Ives* John Hobson Matthews gives a list of place names '. . .with their meanings in English whenever these can be ascertained with tolerable certainty. . .'. Boskerris is translated as 'the habitation by the cherry trees'. Matheson was very particular that a Cornish name he had in mind for the library should be accurate so he consulted no less an authority than Henry Jenner, noted for his *Handbook of the Cornish Language*. Jenner gave him an erudite dissertation on elements of the Cornish language and suggested the name Boskerris Vean which Matheson adopted.

He had a close association with *The St. Ives Times* and as a good friend of Martin Cock the Editor and proprietor, was a regular contributor of verses and humorous articles as well as helping out with editing on occasions. One of his pieces, written under the pen-name M.A.H., in which he set out to prove that the plays attributed to Shakespeare were actually written by a St. Ives man, one John Beckerleg, was the subject of an article in *The St. Ives Times & Echo* on 2nd June 1995, and even more recently M.A.H.'s theory has been challenged by a *Times & Echo* correspondent in Australia.

His 1925 Christmas supplement, for which he wrote to his numerous friends and contacts for letters about St. Ives, produced interesting responses. Many of his pieces were tongue-in-cheek commentaries on current affairs and the activities of the St. Ives Town Council and its members, always amusing but never vindictive.

He produced two books of his local verses, both published by James Lanham, *Crooked Streets. St. Ives Streets in Rhyme* and *Painters, Poets - and others - in St. Ives*. The first was described in one review as 'Bright and breezy poetical description of those fascinating twisted and roughly-paved thoroughfares of St. Ives which will appeal to all who have made acquaintance with that famous West Country town', and it had the following foreword by Hilaire Belloc:

"You will have noted in your travels how the Crooked Streets gather names to themselves which are as individual as they, and which are bound up with them as our names are with all our own human reality and humour. Crooked Streets will never tire a man, and each will have its character, and each will have a soul of its own. To proceed from one to another is like travelling in a multitude or mixing with a number of friends".

It was enhanced by delightful illustrations by Matheson's friend, fellow thespian and one-time President of the St. Ives Arts Club, Capt. Francis Roskruge.

A reviewer in the *Cornishman* had this to say of *Painters, Poets etc.*

'. . .Greville E. Matheson *offers us diversion and entertainment. . . He knows the St. Ives artists and their haunts, their works and idiosyncrasies as but few; and he not only has the pen of a ready writer, but a light and pleasant touch. . ."*

Among the letters of appreciation he received was one from Mr. Tregarthen who asked for an extra copy as the condition of the one he had in the waiting room of his dentist's surgery on the Terrace showed it had much use.

The poetic talent of the Matheson clan, going back to his grandfather, was evident in a book of poems by eleven members of three generations of the Matheson family which he produced for private circulation in 1922. It was described by the *Times Literary Supplement* as '. . .just the kind of poetry which thoughtful, sensitive, well-read people write, not first for publication but for the expression of themselves and a means of communication with their relatives. . .'.

Another book of poems, called: *Ships and Supermen*, was published in 1922 — it was a prolific year. Although the verses were written some years earlier, publication was delayed until Mattheson retired as one poem poked fun at shipowners who attended Conferences at many places on the Continent, and who, he made out, had a very good time. However, Sir William Noble (later Lord Kirkley) who wrote the foreword, saw no cause for apprehension! In his foreword Sir William wrote: 'Recent years have brought home to the nation the fact referred to by Mr. Matheson that, however changed in dress and language, the old sea-sense, the old masterful dominance, is alive in the officers and men of the Mercantile Marine. . ,' a sentiment put to the test a year later in the lifeboats of SS *Trevessa*. The book cover was by Will Owen who illustrated many of W.W. Jacobs' stories as well as Union Castle in-house material for their ships. Owen's work also provides an interesting link with *Trevessa*. In July 1923 the British survivors came home from Mauritius in the Union Castle ship *Goorhka*, the officers in the First Class Saloon, the others in the Second Class Saloon. I have recently seen one of the menu cards for the dinners enjoyed by a survivor which is in the possession of his family. The names of the passengers are printed on the back, and on the front in addition to the lengthy list of courses there is an attractive colour illustration by Owen.

A popular pastime in the 1920's was the composition of 'patchwork poems' in which a thirty line poem had to be constructed using single lines from the works of living poets. In the competition in the journal *The Weekly Westminster* at Christmas 1923 Matheson won the first prize with lines from poems by Hilaire Belloc, Eden Philpotts, W.B. Yeats, Sir Henry Newbolt, John Masefield and Walter de la Mare among others.

In 1934 he produced a little booklet, dedicated to his daughter and three grandchildren, consisting of 50 letters he had selected from the vast number he had received during his lifetime. These were selected, not so much for their content, but for the interesting people who wrote them and his description of the circumstances in which he was involved with them. Among them were Octavia Hill, Coleridge-Taylor, Margaret Kennedy, E. Phillips Oppenheim, Havelock Ellis, C. Lewis Hind and W.W. Jacobs, to mention a few.

Nearer home there was one from Crosbie Garstin regarding a meeting with W.W. Jacobs. Matheson recalls having talked with Garstin after a Saturday night play at the Arts Club. Garstin had finished his latest book the day before and was looking forward to going off the next day on a yachting holiday around the Cornish coast, a holiday which ended in tragedy when Garstin drowned.

When Matheson and his family went to live at Carbis Bay it was not in the Borough of St. Ives but part of Lelant Parish. Before the arrival of the railway it was known as Carbis, consisting broadly of three hamlets, Chy-an-Gweal, Carbis Water and Longstone. The name Carbis Bay was applied to the railway station by the railway company who did not think that Barrepta, the name of the cove, would slip easily off the tongues of their up-country passengers and it was then adopted for the whole of the area. There was a strong community spirit in Carbis Bay into which Matheson and his wife entered with enthusiasm.

To bring out the best in people there is a need for an incentive, and the incentive in Carbis Bay at that time was the need for a community hall. Social activities had been held in the dining room of Mr. Payne's tea gardens until 1922 when the Institute was built in Trencrom Lane. There was a great deal of theatrical talent among the residents and this was put to good use for fund raising for the Institute and eventually the Memorial Hall. Groups called the Carbis Bay Pierrots and the Carbis Bay Players put on plays, shows and pantomimes, to which the Matheson family contributed their talents. He wrote scripts, acted and sang, while his wife, who was a professional musician and had taught Walford Davies, played the piano. Among Carbis Bay residents who came under notice in the reviews were two young lads — Master Dicon Nance and Master T. Scott-Brown.

At the Carbis Bay Institute in February 1923 the Carbis Bay Amateur Dramatic Society put on three performances each consisting of three original plays, one by Matheson's brother-in-law C.J. Pugh, one by R. Moreton Nance and the third by Matheson himself. He acted and his daughter, Mrs. Reed, was one of the first violins. At that time there was poverty and hardship in St. Ives, with children going to school without any breakfast and going hungry to bed. A Local Relief Fund was set up by the Mayor, and the Carbis Bay Players generously agreed to put on a special performance with the proceeds going to the Fund. *The St. Ives Times* put the situation into context when the Editor said that '. . .£10 per week would mean that no man, woman or child in St. Ives need starve. . .'

Matheson was closely associated with the activities of the St. Ives Arts Club and the St. Ives Dramatic Society. In a playbill for a triple performance at the Palais de

Danse in April 1927 he took part alongside familiar names such as Cecil Drage, Gerald Cock and Philip Chellew. The profits went to the St. Ives Nursing Association. In February 1928 another bill announced performances of Barrie's *Dear Brutus* in which he took part, the profits on that occasion going to the Fire Engine Fund. In March 1928 a sketch written and produced by Matheson was performed at the Arts Club. It had only two characters representing St. Ives and Carbis Bay — *The Rivals (not by Sheridan)*. Each tried to outdo the other until the unwelcome siren voices of Penzance and West Penwith offstage brought them together to make common cause. The sketch was notable for its use of the names of local families and places, and was printed in the *St. Ives Times* on April 6th 1928.

Stage performances were not confined to the Palais or the Arts Club. In his book of 50 letters Matheson recalled a picnic known as a 'Phantom Party' got up by the St. Ives artists in 1924 at which every guest, man or woman, had to be dressed in white. The evening began about 8 o'clock with an open-air cabaret on a small stage in Mrs. Ashton's garden at Hawke's Point, and afterwards (with intervals for several suppers) they danced on the small lawn till the early morning. About 5 o'clock some adventurous spirits clambered down the cliffs and bathed. An account by M.A.H. was printed in *The St. Ives Times* and is reported in more detail by Marion Whybrow in her book *St. Ives 1883-1993 Portrait of an Art Colony* (Antique Collectors Club 1994). Mrs. Ashton was well-known as a dowser, and later at Boskerris Vean she demonstrated her art to Matheson. She discovered a spring, but as it was in the middle of the tennis lawn its potential was not exploited.

Greville Ewing Matheson died in 1939 and is buried in the churchyard at Lelant. His family moved to a smaller dwelling and the house and library in Trencrom Lane became two dwellings. They are still occupied and retain the names Boskerris and Boskerris Vean as well as the granite block at the entrance bearing the Cornish words meaning 'In Cornwall I shall have a home as long as I may live'.

I have no doubt that Matheson would have been delighted if he could have foreseen that his booklets about St. Ives, its painters, poets and others, published by James Lanham, would be the forerunners of the extensive lists of local interest books which now appear in *The St. Ives Times & Echo*. If he were alive today he would certainly be a contributor to this Library Supplement.

During his lifetime national and local reviews of his books and his stage work spoke favourably of his talents, but I have yet to find an obituary. Surprisingly *The*

St. Ives Times carried no obituary or acknowledgment of his contribution to the local community despite his association with the paper over many years, although the last of his poems to be printed carried the information that it was contributed on the day before his death. His death is also not referred to in the records of the Savage Club, to which he was elected as a member in January 1898. He is, however, included in the British Biographical Archive with an entry from *The Anglo-African who's who* of 1910, and in Marion Whybrow's book previously mentioned.

Some of his work will reappear from time to time in *The St. Ives Times & Echo*, and I would like to think that if he had a choice of something by which he would be remembered he might have chosen the following poem which concludes his book *Ships and Supermen:*

L'Envoi

A small house granite-grey,
Cool for an August day.
Within cosy and bright,
Meet for a winter night.
Windows large to espy
The green lands, the blue sky.

A hearth both wide and low
For logs to flame and glow.
Books all round on the walls,
Ready when twilight falls,
And lamps are lit, and rain
Whips at the window pane
And the loud wind goes by

Out of an angry sky.
A garden with still ways,
Where one may work and praise.
Sunshine or winter fire,
Such is my heart's desire.
If skies be grey or blue,
Such is my dream come true.

★ ★ ★

The cover of *Ships and Supermen* by Greville E. Matheson was illustrated by 'W.O'. Matheson had an interesting habit of filing any correspondence relating to his books by glueing the letters onto the end papers. Glued into the front of this edition is one letter to Matheson, which reads:

Dear Cornishman, - Many thanks for 'Ships and Supermen' which has just arrived. I can't help feeling from the public purchasers' point of view you have too many shipping advertisements. Of course you have done that to cut down on the expenses but it's bound to have an effect on the public sales I think. It's too late now of course but how nice it would have been to have had a small illustration by me to each poem but there again the enormous expense! I should like to hear how the little book does in spite of these criticisms of mine – With Kindest Regards, Will Owen.

Although there is no acknowledgment in the book it would, in all probability, seem clear that Will Owen was the illustrator of this cover. The letter bears a St. Ives address but details of this artist seem very scant.

★ ★ ★

The following was not included in the Colour Supplement but is included here as an example of Matheson's humorous touch.

Matheson was a frequent contributor to the *St. Ives Times*. These are his interpretations of Shakespeare's possible comments relating to the aspirations of artists in St. Ives when sending their paintings to London in the hope of acceptance by the Royal Academy 1920's — 1930's.

"Will you walk with me about the town?"   *Comedy of Errors*

"So famous, so excellent in art, and still so rising"   *Henry VI*

"A little Academe, still and contemplative in living art"   *Love's Labour Lost*

"All the walls with painted imagery"   *Richard II*

"Look here upon this picture and on this"   *Hamlet*

"Now for London"   *Henry VI*

"I will write all down – such and such pictures"   *Cymbeline*

"There stand the cases"   *Henry VI*

"Toward London they do bend their course"   *Richard III*

"One of them contains my picture; if you choose it then I am yours"

Twelfth Night

"A piece of painting which I do beseech you to accept"

Timon of Athens

"Tis my picture, refuse it not"   *Twelfth Night*

"Come, hang them on the line"   *The Tempest*

"I hope all will be well. We must be patient"   *Hamlet*

"Oft expectation fails, and most oft there where most it promises"

All's Well that Ends Well

"The end crowns all"   *Troilus and Cressida*

"And on that very line standest thou"   *Henry IV*

"I thank thee, Good News! Good News! Ha! Ha!"   *The Merchant of Venice*

"What news then in your paper? The blackest news that ever thou heardest"

Two Gentlemen of Verona

"I am declined"   *Othello*

"Sadly I survive"   *Henry IV*

DIGGING up the DIGEY
fact or fancy?

The Digey is one of the best known streets in St. Ives and seeing the gas engineers digging up the granite setts in November made me think of a group of local worthies who expended much mental energy, and not a little acrimony, on efforts to dig up the origins of the name. This happened over 100 years ago, and we turn to the pages of the *St. Ives Weekly Summary* of 1890 for our information.

The whole thing was sparked off by a tragedy which occurred in the Digey itself. On Monday 18th November 1889 Mr. Samuel Barber left his home in the Digey, having said goodbye to his wife and five small children before joining a local trading vessel as a member of the crew. During the night the house caught fire. Mrs. Barber and two children were rescued, but despite desperate attempts to reach the other three they perished in the blaze. These days the tragic events would have been seen on breakfast TV the following morning, with graphic pictures of the smouldering ruins and eyewitness accounts. Mr. Barber's ship would have been contacted by radio and special arrangements made to get him home. As it was, the first the unfortunate man knew of the tragedy was when he was travelling home by train several days later and read about it in a newspaper left behind by a fellow traveller.

As so often happens in the aftermath of such events deficiencies were brought to light; the fire engine was on the scene some time before the hose could be connected with the fire plug because no one present knew how to do it; the fire hose was kept locked in the town hall instead of being with the engine; the bell used to raise the alarm could not be used as the rope was missing. The situation was not helped by the fact that the bell used to raise the alarm was also used to remind Councillors of their need to attend Council meetings. It seems to have been some time before they sorted out the alarm problem as in the *Weekly Summary* for October 31st 1908 the Boys Brigade officers were asked not to allow the lads to blow their bugles on the terraces at night as there was apparently very little (if any) distinction between the Fire Brigade bugle and the Boys Brigade bugle, and the youngsters should be cautioned about alarming the inhabitants unnecessarily.

So where does the origin of the name Digey come in? In January 1890 the *Weekly Summary* reprinted a letter from the *Western Antiquary* in which the correspondent referred to the inquest on the victims and the frequent references to the name Digey, and asked if anyone could throw any light on the origins of the curious name. The Editor mentioned that a year or two earlier a member of the Penzance Antiquarian Society had suggested that it came from the Cornish *Landithy* meaning Mercy, based on the unsupported tradition that an Abbey had once existed there. Readers were asked if they could help and the correspondence rolled on for several weeks.

First in the field was the Vicar, Rev. Balmer-Jones, with a tongue-in-cheek letter designed to stir up discussion. A further letter appeared in the *Western Antiquary* suggesting the name came from *Diganway* probably meaning a way-road hidden between banks. The Editor thought this was reasonable as in the old days the Digey ran between the hill rising to Barnoon and the sand-banks stretching away to the Island, upon which the lower part of the town - Downlong- had been built. The Vicar came back with a reference in Jago's *Cornish Glossary and Dictionary* in which Digey is shown as farmstead, possibly referring to a farm at Chy-an-Chy, extending to the Meadow.

This stimulated the big guns, starting with Mr. John Hobson Matthews, who at that time was working on his celebrated *History of St. Ives, Lelant, Towednack and Zennor* for which he had access to the town records. Mr. Matthews was not convinced by the Jago explanation and said that he had found nothing in his examination of the early records of the town which would throw any light on the origins of the name. At least he offered no fancy theories.

Next was Mr. W. Tolmie Tresidder, Clerk to the Justices, who had a map on which the Digey was called Digey Street. He also had the deeds for the first house on the left as you enter the Digey (presumably from Fore Street). This house, he said, was formerly of some pretension, had been rebuilt on old foundations and was commonly known as the Dye House, so that the street became Dye House Street. Dye became Di, and the Cornish for house is Chy, so Dye House became Di-chy, which became Digey. Ingenious? The dyeing activity was attributed to barking of nets and sails, although, again, there was no evidence to support the suggestion that barking took place in that part of the town. Mr. Tresidder suggested a return to the name Dye-chy or Di-chy Street, but apparently there were no seconders.

Give him his due, Mr. Tresidder did at least put forward some suggestions. The next was that Virgin Street was a corruption of Verging or Diverging Street because it led off the Digey. He also did not agree that the Digey necessarily led to The Meadow which was not part of a farm at Chy-an-Chy but part of Barn-a-Woon or Barnoon Estate. It would have led to Porthmeor beach, then by footpath along the edge of the cliff to Ventnor well, the only watering place for the locality until 1844 when the Belliars water was brought into the town. (All contemporaneous spellings). Back came Mr. Matthews, who, while finding Mr. Tresidder's comments interesting threw out his Di-chy suggestion as it would hardly be likely that a word would be formed using half English and half Cornish elements. Try again please.

Not to be outdone by Mr. Matthews' knowledge of philology, Mr. Tresidder pointed out the union of English and Cornish in Street-an-Pol and Street-an-Garrow, and that perhaps St. Ives folk were a law unto themselves with a language of their own. The Vicar joined in again, pointing out that the only fact so far produced was that the house for which Mr. Tresidder held the deeds was called the Dye House and he demolished the suggestion that it had to do with barking. Local knowledge, he said, was that the house had been a dwelling owned by the Stephens family for generations, and this seemed to support the theory that it was called Di-chy, later corrupted to Dijey, then Digey. By now each correspondent sought to justify his pet theory. Both Mr. Matthews and Mr. Tresidder came back with broadsides against the Vicar who subsequently admitted he had been talking about the wrong house!

Mr. Matthews had given up, and in his History, published two years later in 1892 he merely says *'derivation uncertain'*. He also quoted extracts from the diary of Capt. John Tregerthen Short who recorded on 29th August 1828 the arrival of the Dutch ship *Enterprise* with Portuguese refugees on board. Mr. Matthews says they were grandees who had escaped Don Pedro's war. They sailed in singing, with guitars and mandolins playing, and were lodged in cellars in the Digey, an appropriate lodging place if, as the gentleman from Penzance suggested in the first place, the name Digey was associated with Mercy. If they were grandees they may well have been lodged in Mr. Tresidder's '. . .house of some pretension . . .'. On the other hand, Mr. Matthews may have got it wrong. They could have been strolling players looking for the big break, and while waiting for their application for political asylum and work permits to be processed they formed a group called The Grandees, earning their keep with live music in the back bar of the Victory Inn across the road, except, of course, on Sunday when they may have augmented the musicians at one of the local Chapels.

The most entertaining letter came from a correspondent who was coy about giving his name but thought that although people laughed at Mr. Tresidder's suggestion, Virgin Street was in fact called Diverging Street. His theory was that DIVERGING STREET had been painted on a board and fastened at the corner of the street. A boy threw stones and knocked off the DI and the final G, leaving VERGIN STREET. VERGIN was near enough to VIRGIN for practical purposes so it became known as VIRGIN STREET. Meanwhile, the letters DI and G which had been knocked off were picked up and fixed on the wall around the corner and the intelligent populace pronounced it as Dye-jee. Many present-day visitors pronounce it Dig-ee.

With that last suggestion the correspondence fizzled out. Everyone had had a bit of entertainment, but in the end no one was really any the wiser as to the origin of the name Digey, and I doubt whether anyone has got any further. The only hope is that perhaps in the Muniments Room in the stately home of a former aristocratic landowner, in a trunk in someone's attic, or among house deeds in a solicitor's office, there may be dusty records tied up with red tape which one day will reveal some facts to go with the fancies. One thing is pretty certain — I bet the gas engineers didn't find any concrete evidence among the granite setts.

THE LEGACY of SELINA, COUNTESS of HUNTINGDON in ST. IVES

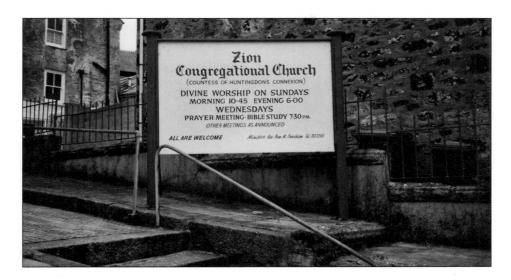

During the summer, when the visitors are in town, if you stand at the gates of Zion — not the heavenly gates but those in front of Zion chapel in Fore Street — you can bet your boots that within a few minutes you will hear someone say "Oh look! What a strange name for a church. Who was the Countess of Huntingdon, and why do they spell Connexion with an x?". You will also hear "Oh look! Salubrious Place — what a pretty name". What our visitors don't know is that they are speaking of a remarkable woman whose visit to St. Ives over two hundred years ago changed the face of Fore Street, created Salubrious Place as we now know it, and whose life's work still has repercussions today.

Selina, Countess of Huntingdon, was born Selina Shirley, on August 24th 1707. Her family were of noble rank, tracing their lineage back to the days of Edward the Confessor. Her grandfather, Sir Robert Shirley, was created Viscount Tamworth and Earl Ferrers in 1711, and her father succeeded to the title in 1717. Selina was an intelligent and serious-minded girl, who had little enthusiasm for the social round and the excesses of the aristocratic circles in which she was expected to move. On June 3rd 1728 she married Theophilus, the ninth Earl of Huntingdon, whose family was even more noble than the Shirley's, having close links with royalty which went back to a Plantagenet prince, Duke of Clarence, brother to Edward IV.

As Countess of Huntingdon, Selina was expected to move even more in court and high society circles, but she much preferred the quiet woods and parks of the Huntingdon estate in Warwickshire, where she could study her bible and engage in good works for the families of the estate workers. Following an illness when she was about 31, she experienced conversion to the Christian faith, and from that time until she died in 1791 at the age of 84, she devoted her life, her energy, her fortune and her position, to proclaiming her new-found faith, a course of action which produced enemies as well as devotees.

Her interest was particularly among those Congregationalists who had left, or been evicted from, the established church following the passing of the Act of Uniformity in 1662. She set up an evangelical training college, Trevecca in Wales, which eventually was to form the basis of Jesus College, Oxford. She was much involved with work among American Indians and the slaves in the southern states of the USA. In 1792 some 2,000 slaves went to Sierra Leone, on the west coast of Africa, where a colony of freed slaves had been formed, many of whom had experienced Selina's ministering work in the USA. Descendants of those slaves in Sierra Leone still worship in Countess of Huntingdon's chapels, and the St. Ives chapel has working links with them.

Selina travelled extensively in England, accompanied by her student preachers, visiting Congregationalists, spreading the Word, and using her resources to provide chapels and ministers. Her friend, George Whitefield, suggested she should visit Cornwall, and her reasons for doing so are best summed up in her own words in a letter to one of her students:

> *". . . My call here is to the tinners and thousands and tens of thousands of poor perishing creatures whom all seem to neglect; their souls are the object of my loving care, and, if the Lord permit, I wish to make three or four establishments in the heart of the tin mines for their instruction and salvation . . .".*

The tinners of Cornwall had a reputation for being rough and tough. John Wesley, on his visits to St. Ives had a rough ride and his meetings were broken up by riotous behaviour. Selina, however, was not daunted by the stories she heard and in 1775, while on her travels in Cornwall, she visited St. Ives, which was in such a bad state that she determined that a chapel was needed and that Robert McAll, one of her students who was accompanying her, should be the minister.

The poor perishing creatures of Cornwall were not the only ones to merit her attention. Selina also set her sights on the souls of the upper classes in Bath, who were more inclined to the activities of Beau Brummel and his circle, and it was there that in 1765 she opened '. . .a splendid chapel . . .'. Attendance at services was by invitation. The Rev. John Penrose, Vicar of St. Gluvias (Penryn) with Budock, writing to his children in Cornwall from Bath, gives interesting accounts of his visits to the brand-new meeting house, and mentions the rumours circulating in Bath that the Countess had '. . . squandered away a great deal more than the Annuity upon Vagabond Preachers, and places for them to preach in . . .'.

So far as Cornwall is concerned, she assembled no less than twenty congregations at different places in the County, regularly ministered to by her chaplains and students. To appreciate the situation in St. Ives at that time it is necessary to go back to the Act of Uniformity in 1662. Clergy who were evicted and lay persons who withdrew from the established church were called Dissenters. In that year Joseph Sherwood was evicted from the living of St. Hilary, but he continued preaching to the congregations of Dissenters alternately at St. Ives and Penzance. At St. Ives he worked with Charles Morton, a noted academic, who had been ejected from the living at Blisland. Morton fell out of favour with the authorities, migrated to New England in 1686 and became the first Vice-President of Harvard College. A variety of ministers followed Sherwood until about 1770 when the work at St. Ives was abandoned. The Exeter Visitation Books of 1774/1775 reported twenty families as Dissenters at St. Ives, with a meeting-house under the pastorage of John Howe, and it seems likely that they would have been the people Selina met when she visited the town in 1775. The location of their meeting-house is not known, although it is thought it may have been somewhere at the bottom of Barnoon Hill.

Apparently there had been a meeting house in the town long before Selina's visit, but when the news of Sir Cloudesley Shovel's victories at Barcelona in 1705 and at Toulon in 1707 reached the town, there were great rejoicings, and it was said that one way in which the inhabitants expressed their gratitude for Sir Cloudesley's achievements, was to tear down the little Presbyterian chapel!

Although Selina decided in 1775 that a chapel should be provided at St. Ives and that Robert McAll would be the minister, it was not until 1799 that Mr. McAll arrived in the town to make the arrangements. Why it took so long for this to happen is not clear, but we know that in 1789 when one of Selina's chapels was opened at Coleford in the Forest of Dean, the Rules of Membership were signed by Mr. McAll who was then based at Gloucester.

In 1802 he purchased from Catherine Hawkings for £120 premises on the site of the present chapel, described as '. . . an old and large fish-cellar, with salt house adjoining and dwelling house over, the latter in a dilapidated and ruinous state . . .'. The premises could not have been entirely ruinous as one room was let to Amey Crane. In 1824 a deposition by an elderly member of the congregation referred to the property as 'Le Malle's fish cellar', and the name Le Malle or Lemal, takes us back to the early 1600's. We hear much these days of boat people from Vietnam and Haiti, seeking refuge from persecution, but in the early 1600's St. Ives was a safe haven for boat people from Brittany - Huguenots, French Protestants, who settled in the town and according to the Borough Accounts received financial help from the townspeople. John Hobson Matthews, in his *History of St. Ives*, refers to one of these as Jean Lemal, a Breton fisherman who married Christian (Kitty) Botterell. The Botterells owned property in the town and it could be that Jean Lemal rented the fish cellar or acquired it through his marriage. Jean was drowned in the Bay, leaving Kitty to bring up their eight daughters in a house at Carn Glaze, referred to in early documents as the Breton house.

On the face of it the site in Fore Street seems an odd place for a fish cellar as there was only a pedestrian access, unsuitable for horse and carts, but the discovery of barrels and fish scales in the foundations during later rebuilding supports the description. It was also not a particularly good place for a meeting-house as it was concealed from Fore Street by two small cottages, which adjoined the present house no. 42. The approach from Fore Street was by a narrow alley. Described as 'insanitary and dangerous', it also provided access to gardens and fields which surrounded the cellar.

Mr. McAll, however, evidently succeeded in getting the cellar into shape as a meeting-house, while the salt house became a home for the minister. In 1804 the title to the property was transferred from McAll to a group of local trustees made up of chapel members. McAll left St.Ives in 1813, and for several years afterwards the chapel languished, to the extent that in 1821 it was in danger of being closed, and was kept going only with the help of the Cornwall Congregational Association and local preachers.

In May 1823 Rev. Thomas Stevenson arrived, and so began a period of intense activity. Stevenson inherited a burden of debt and in November of that year the property and the accumulated debt were transferred from the local trustees to the Countess of Huntingdon's Connexion (with an 'x'), a group of trustees or executors established before her death by Selina to continue her evangelical work and to administer the properties.

From 1823 to 1827 Stevenson worked at extending the membership and acquiring parcels of land surrounding the chapel for enlargement of the building and provision of a Sunday School. Writing to the Secretary of the Trustees in February 1824 he said:

'. . . I desire to be thankful for all the encouragement that the Lord has given me in my labours here, tho' I am often grieved at the little good that appears, but taking all things into consideration much has been done, for in all probability the place would have been shut up; but instead of which there is a house full of hearers. Thirty persons are united in Christian fellowship and 120 children upon an average are taught every Lord's Day, besides the good that is doing in two villages, where I have continued to preach during the winter, at both of which I have steady congregations of about the average of 60 persons, besides children, which at one place are numerous . . .'.

The two villages are not named, but could well have been Hellesveor and Halsetown.

Mr. Stevenson would no doubt have had strong views on Sunday trading. In an earlier letter in October 1823 he wrote:

'. . . There was a tolerably large catch of pilchards on last Friday, about 1500 hogsheads, which caused a sad profanation of the Lord's Day. The chapel was almost deserted both by adults and children. There were not more than 50 children present when I might have expected 150. The congregation bore about the same proportion. On enquiry there seems no absolute need to bring the fish on shore on the Lord's Day. I have already lifted up my voice against it and purpose doing it more particularly . . .'.

In 1882 the woodwork of the chapel roof was examined and found to be in a dangerous state, requiring immediate repairs. Work started in July 1883, but while the roof was open, heavy rain caused the whole thing to collapse, resulting in extensive damage to the interior seats and fittings, while the Minister and the carpenter, who were aloft at the time, were lucky to escape with their lives. A new roof and interior were required — in effect a rebuild — and it was decided the opportunity should be taken to buy the two small cottages so that they could be demolished and the frontage opened up to Fore Street. The chapel was re-opened in August 1884 and the new frontage completed in July 1885 in the form we see today. This, of course, involved the closure of the narrow alley and diversion to the present route up the steps to Salubrious Place which derived its name from Salubrious House, further up the hill, an area where the atmosphere was more salubrious than in the street below.

Sadly, times have changed since the days when Selina travelled the country and established her meeting-houses up and down the land. The 'splendid chapel' at Bath houses an art gallery, while with declining and ageing memberships others have been sold to make way for supermarkets and other developments, and in Cornwall the chapel in St. Ives is the only one still in use.

The chapel in Fore Street is one of the few remaining memorials to an exceptional lady, so the next time you pass the gates of Zion, pause for a moment and try to visualise the scene as it might have been when Selina picked her way along Fore Street in 1775. No Salubrious Place, no view of chapel or fish-cellar, but two small cottages with a smelly alley adjoining. If, on a visit to St. Ives, you attend a service at Zion, spare a thought for the lady who started it all; for Mr. McAll and Mr. Stevenson, coping with the spiritual, financial and physical problems; for those who followed and worked against great financial odds to keep the chapel afloat; for Jean Lemal and those who laboured in the fish-cellar and the salt house, and particularly for those St. Ives people, the Dissenters of 1662, who held fast to their beliefs and formed the first congregations, and whose stream of faith has flowed for more than 300 years.

Perhaps next summer, if you hear someone asking: "Who was the Countess of Huntingdon?", you may be tempted to tell them, but be warned — an answer to one question can lead to another. I have just been asked: "What's all this about the Act of Uniformity?" Ah well, here we go again!

ST. IVES & the SWINDON CONNECTION

Plans were recently announced for a mega-shopping mall to be built at Swindon on the site of the former Great Western Railway Locomotive, Carriage and Wagon Works, another example of inward investment by the Americans. To many people the name Swindon conjures up the vision of 'King' class locomotives, the 'Cornish Riviera Express' and the humble 45XX class tank engines which worked the St. Ives branch, but to those of us St. Ives folk who are a little past the first flush of youth 'Swindon' recalls the period in July previously known as 'Swindon Week', when St. Ives was taken over by GWR workers and their families from Swindon on their annual holiday. We called them 'Swindoners' but they referred to themselves as 'Swindonians'.

This was a week (later extended to a fortnight) when gardeners in the town expected rain, and the evening air would be redolent with the aroma of freshly-caught mackerel being fried for supper in houses where landladies offered 'rooms and attendance'. The visitors arrived on their special train early on Thursday morning, an arrival watched by crowds of local people on the Malakoff, with similar crowds going to see them off when they left for home. I never saw the arrivals, but recall being taken to the Malakoff for the departures.

At that time I had no knowledge of Swindon Works and certainly no idea that in future years as a Great Western man myself I would be involved in the complex arrangements which enabled those families to come to St. Ives, and I doubt if any of those happy holidaymakers gave a thought to the fact that their town, their jobs and their holiday were the outcome of a decision taken by two young men in 1840.

When Isambard Kingdom Brunel at the age of 27 planned his railway from Bristol to London he ordered locomotives from a number of builders, and as the railway progressed there was a need for a depot where they could be maintained and repaired. He asked his Locomotive Engineer, Daniel Gooch aged 21, to investigate and report on a suitable location. In his diary for 1840 Gooch said: '*I reported in favour of Swindon, it being the junction with the Cheltenham branch and also a convenient division of the Great Western line for engine working. Mr. Brunel and I went to look at the ground, then only green fields, and he agreed with me as to its being the best place.*'

The reference to 'the convenient division . . . for engine working' referred to the intention at that time to use engines of Gooch's *Firefly* class with 7ft driving wheels on the level section between London and Swindon and smaller ones with 6ft drivers on the Swindon to Bristol section with its heavy inclines at Box and Wootton Bassett. In the event the *Firefly* class locomotives worked through to Bristol and were the backbone of the GWR passenger service for many years.

It was said that on their visit Brunel and Gooch discussed the subject while taking a picnic lunch alongside the railway and threw a stone which would mark the site of the new depot. Whether or not this is true the site was approved and the Works were built. The machinery was started on 28th November 1842 and the Works put into regular operation on 2nd January 1843. The first locomotive to be built at Swindon was completed in thirteen weeks early in 1846, and in subsequent years Swindon Works acquired a reputation for quality and craftsmanship which produced some of the finest locomotives in the world.

The Works site was about two miles from Swindon, at that time a small market town, and to accommodate the workers a railway town known as New Swindon grew up around the Works. New Swindon and old Swindon were formally linked in 1900. In 1841 the population was 2,459 and by 1935 had reached 65,000, of whom some 12,000 were employed in the railway Works. The GWR directors and managers were much involved in the welfare of their staff and encouraged and supported social and educational activities. One of these at Swindon was the provision of a Library in the Works in 1843. The following year the library became the Mechanics Institution with an initial membership of fifteen '. . . *for the purpose of disseminating useful knowledge and encouraging rational amusement amongst all classes of people employed by the Great Western Railway . . .'*. Among the 'rational amusements' were dancing and theatricals in accommodation specially adapted in the Works themselves. Mr. Gooch (later Sir Daniel Gooch) was the first President of the Institution and Mr. Brunel an honorary member.

In 1849 the Company laid on an excursion for the benefit of the members of the Institution, some 500 people travelling on it, and through the courtesy of the Directors in future years this event developed into an annual feature during the Works holidays, known to GWR staff as 'Swindon Trip' with special trains to many holiday destinations. Weymouth was usually the most popular, closely followed by the West of England and Weston-super-Mare, extending to London and other places such as Barry Island and Blackpool. St. Ives was a popular choice, many families returning year after year to the landladies who became friends and in some cases relatives, while even now children of those visitors return with children of their own.

The arrangements for the 'Trip' took the best part of twelve months to organise. They were put in hand immediately after the return to work from the annual holiday and dealt with by the Mechanics Institution in co-operation with the Staff Department of the Locomotive, Carriage & Wagon Superintendent's office. Each member of the Works staff would be given a form on which to indicate the desired destination for the following year and the number of tickets required for him and his family. These would be analysed into destinations so that the train services required could be assessed. Each year the aim would be to provide the best, most economical services which would not interfere with the normal business.

The year 1936 provides an example of what was involved. After the 1935 holiday forms were issued to some 12,000 staff, which when completed indicated that tickets were required for some 27,000 passengers covering a wide range of destinations. These were compared with the services run in 1935 and a draft programme prepared of the number of trains required for the following year. This draft was passed to the Traffic Superintendent at Bristol for examination in the light of forthcoming timetable plans and the availability of locomotives, coaches and train crews, and discussed at meetings with Traffic Department representatives from the receiving Districts. From these meetings a final plan and timetable for 1936 emerged for about 30 special trains, requiring some 35 locomotives and 500 coaches. Many of these were paint and repair jobs turned out of the Swindon shops and used for the Trip before being released for the summer traffic, but others had to be found within the normal allocations. The long distance trains were not the only consideration. Many of the Works staff lived in the surrounding villages, so arrangements had to be made for special local services to bring them into Swindon. The train working arrangements for the operation would be set out in a printed notice of some 20 to 30 pages.

The administrative work in the Staff Department was considerable, including writing out 12,000 tickets, and for the operation to proceed smoothly passengers were allocated to specific trains to avoid overcrowding on one and a shortfall on another, ensuring that every passenger had a seat. The trains for Weymouth, the

West of England and Wales were assembled in sidings at Rodbourne Lane, to the west of Swindon station, while those for London, the north and the south coast started from sidings outside the Works General Offices, and families arriving for their allocated train had to clamber up temporary wooden steps with their suitcases, buckets, spades and raincoats to set off on their holiday journeys.

The 1936 Trip seems to have gone off very well, judging by this extract from a letter from Mr. W.H. Bickham of 7 Newhall Street, Swindon which appeared in the *St. Ives Times* in July 1936. I hope the seven children he mentions who were the guests of St. Ives at Weymouth enjoyed their day and wonder if any eventually came to St. Ives.

> *'May I, through your columns, express on behalf of Swindonians, our appreciation of the kindly and spontaneous welcome extended by the inhabitants of St. Ives. This very friendly gesture, on the occasion of our annual holiday, very much enhances the pleasure afforded in a visit to your delightful resort, and the ever-increasing numbers, year by year, are due to the many Swindonians who each year return full of enthusiasm in the delights of St. Ives and District.*
>
> *May I also express our sincere thanks to the Carnival Committee and officers and members of St. Ives Cricket Club, in their very kindly gesture towards 'Swindon's Poor Kiddies Outing Fund'. As a result of their efforts, I shall hand over to the Fund the sum of £2, so that St. Ives will have the pleasure of knowing that seven of the children who will travel to Weymouth on Wednesday week, will be the guests of the inhabitants of St. Ives. To all of you I say with all my heart, thank you. Again thanking one and all, and trusting to have the pleasure of renewing many associations next year'.*

Mr. Bickham was not alone in expressing his enjoyment of the attractions of St. Ives. Sir Daniel Gooch himself was a frequent visitor between 1878 and 1883, staying with Lady Gooch at Tregenna Castle Hotel. They were keen walkers and in his diary Sir Daniel referred to their daily walks in the country round about St. Ives and '. . . through the town to the Head and the western sands . . .'

In the late 1950's when I was working in Bristol it fell to my lot on occasions to cover the operation at Swindon from Thursday evening until the departure of the last train on Friday mid-morning, to liaise with the Works staff and Traffic Control at Bristol and to deal with any emergencies. Following the departure of the night trains there was the chance of an hour or two's sleep on the settee in the Station Master's office before the arrival of the first Friday passengers at about 4 o'clock in the morning. It must be said that apart from events which were unforeseeable such as an engine failure or a derailment the operation invariably went off smoothly because of the meticulous planning by all departments involved. The main anxiety was the weather. The sidings were in the open and in 1907 the GWR Magazine reported all went well but '. . . *the extraordinary downpour of rain just about the time of departure will long be remembered by Swindonians generally, and particularly by the individuals who were unfortunate enough to be out of cover . . .*'.

When Swindon Works closed its gates and the famous Swindon hooter which regulated the comings and goings of Swindon residents sounded for the last time it was also the end of an era which combined art and technology in the building of beautiful machines. Before too long we will have lost the skills in building steam locomotives which Swindonians had in abundance, but in the meantime I have the privilege of being associated with a number of former Works employees in *The Firefly Trust* in the building of a broad gauge locomotive of the *Firefly* class to the original design of Daniel Gooch. When this is completed and running on broad gauge track in various parts of the country we will think back to those days when Swindon Works was nothing more than green fields, and the town of New Swindon and Swindon Week had not yet been thought of.

It is most unlikely that Brunel and Gooch saw their choice of Swindon in the context of inward investment to the area, but their decision to build their Works where the stone is said to have landed resulted in considerable contributions to the economy of towns like St. Ives and we must be thankful that during their picnic lunch they saw those green fields as the site for what became an internationally renowned Locomotive Works rather than a shopping development.

As a Director of The Firefly Trust *I am delighted that the replica* Firefly *locomotive, built at Didcot to the plans of Daniel Gooch, now runs in steam on original G.W.R. broad gauge rails at the Didcot Centre of the Great Western Society and that much of the work was done by ex-GWR Swindon Works locomotive engineers who were familiar with St. Ives and Swindon Trip. For further information visit the Great Western Society website http://www.didcotrailwaycentre.org.uk*

More on Swindon Week

Verses have been written about towns and cities all over the world and I would have said it was unlikely that any had been written in connection with Swindon but I would have been wrong. The following by Greville Ewing Matheson who lived at Boskerris Vean, Carbis Bay, was contributed to *The St. Ives Times*.

THE LITTLE GIRL FROM SWINDON

I saw her on Tregenna Hill
With basket out a-shopping,
Her shingled hair was waved and bare
And My! She did look topping.
She wore a gauzy dress of blue,
With two white roses pinned on,
Oh! She was neat, and she was sweet,
This little girl from Swindon

I saw her go from shop to shop,
Her savings she was spending,
She shopped with care, and such an air
Of pleasant condescending.
She went home with a box of creams,
A pork-pie and a findon ★
Oh! She was neat, and she was sweet,
This little girl from Swindon

Her eyes were blue as is the sea,
Her smile was wise and merry,
Her little face (of paint no trace),
Was brown as is a berry
And Oh! her stockings, well, well, well!
(There was a roguish wind on!)
Oh! She was neat, and she was sweet,
This little girl from Swindon

★ *Smoked haddock*

PERCY LANE OLIVER O.B.E.

Founder of the voluntary blood donor service

Little did I think when I joined the Cornwall Family History Society on my retirement that membership would lead to the publication of a book on how to trace your railway ancestors, to an exhibition and a book on the first railways in Japan, and to the opportunity of helping to honour the memory of a man who has done more than most of us can ever hope to do in the service of our fellow men, yet is relatively unknown. The first three are stories in themselves, but this article sets out something of the background to the life and work of that remarkable man.

Could you put a name to the man who developed the system of volunteer blood donors which is now accepted as part of our health system? I have asked many people, including members of the medical profession, and while they know who was involved with cancer treatment, vaccination, anaesthetics and penicillin, hardly anyone outside the Blood Transfusion Service recognises the name of Percy Lane Oliver. I knew nothing of him, or the fact that he was born in my home town of St. Ives Cornwall, until I did some work on the transcription of part of the 1881 census involving St. Ives and was asked if I could find some information relating to Oliver's family. From this modest enquiry I found he and I had the same family roots, which kindled the desire to find more about him and to make him more widely known.

Before talking about the man himself, some information on blood donors and transfusion may be helpful. Blood has always had a fascination for the human race. Shakespeare's plays drip with it. Tracker dogs were called bloodhounds, and the Salvation Army incorporated it into its motto Blood and Fire. While the alchemists of old sought to transmute base metals into gold, others were experimenting with the replacement of 'worn-out' blood to treat senility and chronic diseases. In Greek mythology Medea, a magician, wife of Jason of the Argonauts, restored her aged father-in-law to the vigour and sprightliness of youth by drawing away the blood from his veins and filling them again with the juices of certain herbs. Sadly, efforts to find the recipe have been unsuccessful and the potion is not available on the NHS! Attempts were made in the 15th century to rejuvenate Pope Innocent VIII. In 1652 the Rev. Francis Potter, Vicar of Kilmarton in Somerset, experimented with transfusions using a hen. It seems they did not have Medea's success.

It was not until 1818 that human blood was used, by syringe, and by this method casualties were treated in the Franco-Prussian war. In 1900 the four major blood groups were discovered, and in 1914 sodium citrate was found to be the ideal anti-coagulant. The casualties of the First World War gave surgeons opportunities of developing and improving the techniques of transfusion and in this they were helped by the readily available source of donors. Lightly wounded men were invited to act as donors, and rewarded with 14 days in 'Blighty'.

The experience gained in field hospitals was valuable in peacetime, but the post-war problem was the availability of donors. Some surgeons retained their own whom they could call upon on demand and who were paid so much per session, but it was generally a rather hit and miss situation. All this, however, was to change as a result of a telephone call to Percy Lane Oliver in October 1921.

Percy Lane Oliver was born on 11th April 1878 at the home of his grandparents, Paul and Margery Curnow, in Fish Street, St. Ives. Paul Curnow was a blacksmith and relief keeper for Godrevy lighthouse in St. Ives Bay, as well as a highly respected lifeboat cox'n, whose decorations included a medal from Emperor Napoleon III. At the time of Percy's birth the Oliver family lived in Maidenhead, where his father and mother were teachers. The family moved to London around 1883, and in 1892 Percy won a Science and Art Scholarship. In 1893 he passed first in the Civil Service Examination out of 449 candidates, but was rejected by the Medical Board. One wonders how the course of medical history might have been changed if he had been accepted! Following this disappointment he got a job as Assistant Librarian with Camberwell Borough Council in 1893, and in 1901 transferred to the Town Hall staff, where he remained until his retirement. He was a founder member of the Camberwell Division of the British Red Cross and became its Honorary Secretary in 1910.

During the first world war he served in the Royal Naval Air Service, stationed at Crystal Palace, and during his off-duty and leave periods he and his wife engaged in considerable work in connection with refugees, organising and financially managing four refugee hostels in Camberwell. For this he was awarded the O.B.E. in 1918, the presentation being made by King George V personally. On leaving Buckingham Palace after receiving his award onlookers mistook his medal for a VC and chaired him down the road!

In October 1921, in his capacity as Honorary Secretary of the Camberwell Branch of the Red Cross, he received a telephone call from the nearby King's College Hospital. They were in urgent need of a blood donor and sought his help. He and a few colleagues went to the hospital, and from them Sister Linstead, a Red Cross worker, was chosen, becoming the first voluntary blood donor. The results of this exercise so impressed Oliver that mainly with the help of his wife he set about devising and organising a system for a panel of donor volunteers, whose health and blood details were checked by the Hospital and kept on record cards in his home, where there was continuous telephone cover. In the first year there were four members of the panel and they had one call. Five years later there were 400 members and over 700 calls. Oliver was convinced that organised panels of volunteer donors were the answer and he worked hard at setting up similar panels, particularly in London, with the help of groups such as St. John Ambulance, Toc H and the Rover Scouts. To cope with the organisation and the paperwork it was also necessary to move to a larger house! Much of his free time was spent travelling round the country, explaining the system and encouraging the formation of yet more local groups of volunteers.

Although on its inception in 1921 Oliver called it the London Blood Transfusion Service, it was really a voluntary donor service for local hospitals. It progressed to the stage where the official support of the British Red Cross Society was considered essential. This was forthcoming and in 1926 it became the British Red Cross Blood Transfusion Service, later changed to the Greater London Red Cross B.T. Service and eventually developed into the National Blood Transfusion Service which is so familiar to us today. General hospitals were not charged for the service and no payment was ever made to, or expected by, the donors. The expenses of running the organisation from the house in South London were met by charging private clinics, by grants from Institutions, and by Oliver's own efforts.

Oliver had the support of many eminent surgeons and doctors, but there were others who resented this intrusion into medical preserves by a layman. Many donors had to keep their involvement secret from families and employers, and as recently as 1940 Percy Oliver was still travelling the country trying to dispel apprehensions and encourage the supply of donors and the setting up of panels. In February of that year he returned to St. Ives where he gave an illustrated lecture at which the Area Secretary of Toc H asked those present '. . . *not to stand in the way of would-be donors, but rather to go out and radiate the wonderful work that had been done and was being done by blood transfusion. . .*'

Oliver's work attracted attention worldwide and many countries sent representatives who sought and acted upon his advice on setting up similar organisations. In 1937 an exhibition at a meeting of the Voluntary Blood Donors Association featured the idea of stored blood which, although originally used by Canadian doctors in the first war, had been brought to the fore in the Spanish Civil War. This was to become the basis of the war-time blood bank which Oliver helped to create at Luton in 1939. Surprisingly Oliver received no official recognition for his work in the development of voluntary blood donor panels, although in later years he was invited back to the Palace to talk with the King about his work.

Percy Lane Oliver died on 16th April 1944, but his achievements are not forgotten. A memorial consisting of a portrait and a panel with an appropriate inscription was unveiled in the entrance hall of the Haematology Department of King's College Hospital, London in 1972 by Her Royal Highness the Duchess of Gloucester. A framed copy of this is in every Regional Transfusion Centre in Britain,

A photograph of Percy Lane Oliver and a commemorative plaque in the entrance lobby of the Stennack Surgery.

and another is in the Donor Centre in Rome, bearing a suitable translation. In 1979 the Greater London Council provided an appropriate plaque on the house in South London where so much of Oliver's work was undertaken and where his daughter, Mrs. Marjorie Hardy, still lives. Those who worked with him established a Memorial Fund which each year makes an award to a medical or lay nominee, year and year about, in recognition for outstanding service in the field of blood transfusion. This is a prestigious award and recognised as such by those in the business. The Fund also offers modest grants to young scientists involved in appropriate research projects.

While Oliver's work was recognised in London, in Regional Transfusion Centres around the country and in Rome, there was nothing in the town of his birth, and arising from discussions with his daughter, her family, and officers of the Memorial Fund last year, it was proposed that a plaque be erected in St. Ives. It so happened that a new Health Centre was due to open there towards the end of the year, which would provide an ideal location. The concept was warmly supported by the St. Ives Town Council and the Doctors who would be occupying the Health Centre, and on Friday 11th April 1992 a suitably inscribed Cornish granite plaque, accompanied by a portrait, was unveiled by the Mayor in the presence of Lady Limerick, Chairman of the British Red Cross Society, members of Oliver's family and Mr. Frank Hanley, the only living person who worked with Percy Oliver and who for many years was Chairman of the Memorial Fund.

While these memorials remind us of where Oliver was born and where he lived and worked, his greatest memorial is in the voluntary blood donor organisations around the world which he worked so hard to create. So the next time you see a blood transfusion van travelling at speed with its blue light flashing, or when you or a relative have a blood transfusion, spare a thought for Percy Lane Oliver, Sister Linstead and the army of voluntary donors; and if you have the time, see if there is anything you can do to help carry on the work he started.

LETTERS to AMERICA
80 years on

Many folk involved in family history research will have experienced the excitement of finding long-lost or unknown relatives in farflung lands. Last year I was instrumental in getting together families in the UK and America, neither of whom knew of the existence of the others, not through family history but research into construction by British engineers of the first railways in Japan. Nearer home I found in America relatives of my late cousin Mrs. Susie Hosking, better known as Miss Geen. Apart from the pleasure this brought her in the last months of her life it produced an added bonus in the form of letters written from St. Ives some 80 years ago.

Susie's grandmother, Grace Uren, married John Stevens Davies in 1870, and in 1910 three of their sons, Richard, William Henry and Robert, left St. Ives for America. One of the earliest emigrants from Cornwall, Francis Clymo, left Perranzabuloe in 1819 to go prospecting in Maryland, and many thousands followed before the Davies brothers decided to follow their example, not for a lucky strike, but for a regular job of work. Michigan, Montana, California and Nevada were familiar territories to Cornishmen, and no doubt many families in Penwith knew more about activities in Butte, Montana, from letters home, than they did about places in Cornwall. Robert Davies went to California, Richard and William Henry to Arizona.

Arizona came on the scene later than most of the other States, partly due to the Indian problem and the lack of railways. In 1880 the American census indicated some 200 Cornishmen working in Arizona. By the turn of the century the rich copper deposits, particularly in the south-east, were attracting Cornish miners from other parts of America and direct from Cornwall, and places such as Globe, Prescott, Jerome and Bisbee became major mining centres. It was to Globe that Richard and William Henry went and found work in the Old Dominion mine. At that time Globe, some 90 miles east of Phoenix in Gila County — Apache Indian country — was already a major producing area of copper, with the Old Dominion smelter working at least six furnaces. William Henry eventually returned to St. Ives, but Richard stayed on and settled in Globe.

Richard had a son, also called Richard, and it was he whom I traced using the telephone directory in Phoenix when my wife and I visited Arizona last year. Dick Davies, as he is generally known, also worked in the mine at Globe. Although he had been in England as a Lt. Colonel in the U.S. Army during World War 2 his duties in connection with preparations for D-Day prevented him visiting the town where his father had been born in 1894. Dick had in his possession a number of letters written to his father and uncle from St. Ives. Most were from their parents, John and Grace Davies, but some were from their sister Grace, who married Benjamin Geen, and who was Susie's mother. My connection is that my grandmother, Elizabeth Catherine Geen, was Benjamin's sister.

I have been given transcripts of the first batch of these letters and it is hoped that other letters will follow. In the extracts quoted in this article I have retained the spelling as in the originals, as this adds a certain degree of homely charm and it is what was said, not how it was spelt, that matters.

They make fascinating reading and are probably typical of letters written in countless Cornish homes to husbands, sons and brothers all over the world. The only formal thing about them is the standard opening sentence: *'We now take the pleasure of answering your welcome letter. Glad to hear from you all and to hear that you are all well as it leaves us at present, thank God'*. The rest is written just as if they were holding a conversation, and at times it is possible to visualise the writer (usually mother), chewing the end of the pen and wondering what to say next. They were written at roughly monthly intervals, and news of the family is interspersed with news of the town and the fishing, as well as homely advice.

Many contain references to the health of Richard and William Henry's elder brother John Uren Davies. In April 1911 their mother said:

> *'. . . John Uren do say he is much better, but I can't see much difference in him. Think it will be a long time before he do come better by what we can see of him . . .'*

In May it was:

> *'. . . John Uren just the same. He do say he is much better. He always says he is better, glad to hear him say so. All I can say he can move his hands much better and*

70

they do look better than what they have been. He do go out a good bit when it is fine weather . . .'

Presumably he suffered from arthritis and we don't know how much he improved, but he survived another four years before being buried in Barnoon Cemetery overlooking the sea at Porthmeor beach.

Richard and William Henry probably went to Globe at the suggestion of other St. Ives men who had preceded them, some of whom, like William Henry, decided it was not for them. In April 1911 their sister Grace wrote:

'. . . There is a lot of people on the way home. Dicky Ledra is one of them . . .'

Grace, their mother, wrote:

'. . . Bob Beard was up seeing us one day this week and he is getting on fine. He told us a bit of news about you all. But he said he did not like you working in that mine. It was so hot for you and he hopes you have got a better job by this time and so do we. It was very nice to have a chat about you all . . .'

This was followed in July by

'. . . I was telling you in the last letter that John Proddon was home, but his chest did not come home when he did come. But it did arrive home all safe only a week later. The ole chap is looking very well . . .'

It is interesting that Grace should have been concerned about the heat in the mine, but made no comment on the heat at surface, where temperatures reach over 100 degrees. This also makes one wonder how much they knew of the lifestyle of the boys in Globe. Unfortunately no letters from America seem to have survived in St. Ives, which would have given us an idea of their impressions of a land very different from the one they had left. Instead of the sea, the beaches, the cliffs and moors of Penwith they were in a landscape of desert, fantastically shaped rocks, saguaro cactus and vast distances.

Two other men from St. Ives in Arizona in 1912 were John Penberthy and his elder brother Richard. They worked in a mine at Miami, a few miles west of Globe, where Richard was a shift boss. Richard returned home to join the Royal Navy in the First World War, while John joined the US Army but subsequently returned to St. Ives. John's daughter has no letters to or from Arizona, but she does have a super photograph of her uncle Richard, with 161 other miners and an unidentified mine captain from Camborne, together with one of the mules, grouped in front of the mine headworks. From Halsetown, just outside St. Ives, Thomas Martin went to Tombstone where he worked in the Silver Thread mine before being killed in March 1887 when a cage fell on him while he was working in the shaft.

When Richard and William Henry Davies left St. Ives it is likely their only acquaintance with horses was seeing them on the farms on the outskirts of the town, and with carts taking fish to the railway station or selling milk, but in Arizona they were the means of transport. On March 17th 1911 Grace wrote:

> '. . . I hope you have found your horse by this time. I suppose someone has stolen it and if they have I would say you will not see it again. How much money did it cost you? Must be a great loss to you but we hope you have got it by this time . . .'

A month later she was able to write:

> '. . . Glad to hear my dear Richard is getting on so well and have found your horse again . . .'

If those returning from America did so because they had become disillusioned with the prospects, the prospects at home in St. Ives seemed equally bleak — March 1911:

> '. . . I am very sorry to say it is very slight times home here now. The boats were out last night — no fish. And it have been very bad weather, nothing but gales every day. This is the first time the boats have been out for the last three weeks . . .'. In May it was '. . . We have had very bad weather, nothing but gales every day. Many boats have not got a shilling in April and they only went out yesterday, the first time for the week, so you must think what sort of times it is home here at present with the fishermen . . .'

The letters contain information about alterations to roads and houses in the town, including the provision of '. . . a nice hall for skatin and for a place of amusement if wanted . . .'. The 'nice hall' had a chequered existence, as a dance hall with the finest maple floor in Cornwall, then a cinema with the drawback of a flat floor, and finally the studio of the sculptor Dame Barbara Hepworth, where many of her large sculptures were produced.

The first letter was written from Carncrows Street situated in the lower part of the town near the harbour known as Downlong, shortly before John and Grace moved to Chapel Street in the area known as Uplong. Grace said:

'. . . We do like it Uplong very much, a nice little house with five rooms altogether, and we can see a lot more in one day than what we did in one month Downlong. I don't care if I couldn't go Downlong any more . . .'

They were also proud to tell their sons about their latest acquisition, a gramophone:

'. . . Bob Beard told us that you have got a nice gramafone and very nice records. We should like to hear it very much and then we would tell you whether it is a better one than ours. But I think yours cost more money than ours. We got a little one, no horn, but the same sort of records. It did not cost much money but it is very nice for us when we are alone in the evenings . . .'

Although the boys were thousands of miles away, Mother could still give them advice — April 1911:

'. . . My dear William Henry, I heard you do something that I don't like for you to do, that is when you are working you do put cold water over yourself. Don't never do that. It is very dangerous thing to do. It may cost you your life. Don't do it my dear boy, I am telling you for the sake of your life . . .'

It is not known whether William Henry took the advice, but he was 70 when he died at St. Ives in 1957.

In July 1911 the quinquennial Knill festival was held at St. Ives. In his will John Knill made bequests for certain categories of St. Ives people, including an award of £5 to the woman *'. . . deemed to be the best knitter of Dunvargan or any kind of fishing net . . .'*. 'Dunvargan' was a technique which originated in Ireland and produced a net which hung in square meshes. Grace reported that she had:

'. . . put in for the knitting . . ,' but said that *'. . . they shared it up in four, so I only got 25 shillings this time. It is better than nothing, but it do belong to me. I do consider that I am the best in the town. But it seems to me they don't understand the work, so they do what they like now in this day. I ought to have it for I know that I am the best. So it is all over for another five years. I see that my name is not in the paper, so I don't care whether it is or not . . .'*

Her daughter Susie confirmed to me that her mother was in fact very skilled in the knitting technique and was probably right in her conviction that she was the best in the town.

The boys in Globe were very good at sending gifts home to their parents, among them a watch for father, a ring for mother, a pipe for their sister's husband Ben, and handkerchiefs for Susie and her sister. On a visit to St. Ives Uncle Richard gave Susie's sister a gold nugget from Arizona, but sadly it was stolen in a burglary years later. There is, however, one poignant link with those Cornishmen in Arizona, a black shawl, no doubt a gift to Grace from her boys. Tasselled and embroidered with black roses it was worn at Susie's funeral by her great-niece. I am sure that Uncle Richard would have approved.

Letters from America were frequently printed and quoted in the *Cornish Telegraph* newspaper, but letters to America are harder to come by, which make the Davies letters so valuable. Perhaps this article will encourage our American, South African, Australian etc cousins to check out those trunks in the attic and see if any more exist.

D. H. LAWRENCE
U-boats and railway engines off Clodgy Point

Peter Stanier in his article *Some Writers in the Early Years of St. Ives Library* in the Library Centenary Supplement of *The St. Ives Times & Echo* (April 1997) referred to D.H. Lawrence and the suspicions surrounding him and his wife Frieda while they were living at Zennor, followed by their summary eviction from Cornwall. A 'writing and publishing' industry has grown up around Lawrence. His books and letters, as well as books and articles written about him occupy much shelf space in Libraries. Many a PhD has no doubt been obtained on the strength of critical analysis and in-depth interpretation of his writings, but as far as I am aware no-one has yet come up with the official reason why the cottage at Higher Tregerthen was searched and he and his wife were given three days to leave the county. Lawrence himself, writing to his friend Lady Cynthia Asquith said: '. . . *This bolt from the blue has fallen this morning: why, I know not, any more than you do. I cannot even conceive how I have incurred suspicion - have not the faintest notion. We are as innocent even of pacifist activities, let alone spying of any sort as the rabbits in the field outside . . .*'.

Lawrence may not have appreciated that living among the farms and villages of West Penwith would not be quite the same as his experience in Austria, Italy and London. Even in my young days west of Eagle's Nest was foreign parts. A walk to Zennor by the field path was an adventure. A Sunday School outing to Sennen Cove in a charabanc was an event. In 1916 speculation would inevitably have attended the arrival in the area of a known pacifist with a German wife who had high-born German family connections.

His avoidance of the call-up was probably viewed with suspicion despite the fact that he was exempted from military service on health grounds by two separate Military Medical Boards, on the second occasion with category C3, light non-military duties. Local attitudes might have been different if he had made even some modest non-combative contribution to the war effort rather than spend his time writing what were regarded as questionable poems and books (his book *The

Rainbow had been banned as obscene the previous year). It may also be that local people were jealous of the fact that while their men were fighting in France or in the Navy, Lawrence chose to live what they may have regarded as a Bohemian life. They probably also had doubts about his associates who appeared to be avoiding the call-up, including some who may have had connections with the occultist Alesteir Crowley, and of whom Lawrence said in a letter to Lady Cynthia Asquith, '. . . *There are near us some herb-eating occultists: they fast, or eat nettles; they descend naked into old mine shafts, and there meditate for hours and hours upon their own transcendent infinitude; they descend on us like a swarm of locusts, and devour all the food on shelf or board; they even gave a concert, and made the most fearful fools of themselves.*' The concert in August 1917 was in the Pavilion at Porthminster beach and resulted in heated letters in the correspondence columns of *The St. Ives Times*.

The suggestion that Lawrence and his wife were supplying German submarines with fuel and food now seems ludicrous. Apparently there was no evidence of any subversive activity, but Frieda's high-born German family and her correspondence with her mother in Germany through a friend in Switzerland would have been viewed with suspicion, and as someone fearful of internment she herself does not appear to have been very discreet in her comments and actions. They certainly seem to have been careless about concealing lights. In September 1917 *The St. Ives Times* reported that Lawrence's friend Cecil Gray, down the road at Bosigran, had been summoned before the Magistrates at Penzance and fined what was then the substantial sum of £20 for persistent neglect of this requirement. The summons followed the interruption by the military of a convivial evening at Bosigran and the evidence of the Assistant Coast-watching Officer. Ignorance could not be pleaded as a reason for non-observance of the requirements as *The St. Ives Times* printed weekly details of 'Times for Obscuring Lights at St. Ives', with times for lights within view of the sea as well as for other lights. Times were also given at which lights on vehicles were to be lit.

To be fair to the inhabitants of Zennor, they were not the only Cornish folk to have reservations. *The St. Ives Times* of September 6th 1918 carried a report that for a long time feeling had run high in Newquay against aliens being allowed to reside on the sea front. Appeals had been made to the Authorities but no action taken, so the Newquay residents took matters into their own hands. A large number assembled on the Island Estate for speeches and patriotic songs followed by stone throwing at a lodging house supposed to be harbouring aliens, resulting in nearly all the windows being broken. The crowd dispersed when they were told that the aliens had already left.

The war at sea around the coasts of Britain took a dreadful toll of ships and men, and the seabed off the north coast of Cornwall is littered with the remains of ships sunk by U-boats. Their objective was to sink as many allied ships as possible but the attitude towards the crews appears to have varied from one U-boat captain to another. In some cases they waited until ships' boats were clear before firing their torpedoes or setting their scuttling charges. By contrast, in others they abandoned or shot men in the water or shelled the lifeboats. Many reports of sinkings make no mention of the fate of the crew. Some give details of casualties while others report that survivors were rescued by the St. Ives lifeboat, made their way in their ships' boats to local ports, or were picked up by other vessels and landed further afield.

The Admiralty issued weekly returns of arrivals and sailings of merchant ships of all nationalities at or from British ports as well as losses of British merchant vessels by mine or submarine and unsuccessful attacks on British merchant ships. These returns were printed in the local press but while in some weeks they may have shown a reduction in the overall number of ships sunk, increases in specific areas were not revealed. Little else was reported other than inquests on drowned sailors. For example, *The St. Ives Times* of May 24th 1918 reported that Mr. Edward Boase had held an inquest on the bodies of Frederick Charles Dakers, master mariner, aged 46, and J. Stalman, boatswain, aged 58, whose bodies had been landed at St. Ives a few days earlier. Dr. Nicholls said that Dakers was probably drowned following concussion and Stalman had died from fracture of the skull caused by act of the enemy, verdicts being returned accordingly.

Many survivors were landed at St. Ives and the Salvation Army offered them immediate shelter and food before they went on their way. Those who were injured or too ill to be moved the ten miles to hospital were taken into the homes of local people. *The St. Ives Times* for May 17th 1918 carried a report of the gratitude expressed by a ship's Captain for the kindness extended to him and his crew by the inhabitants of St. Ives after they had been landed in the town on May

3rd, especially the Salvation Army who had accommodated them in their hall and given them refreshments. Captain Nicholas Mastroyains, who had been ill with pneumonia since he was landed, extended his personal thanks to Mrs. Ellis of 44 Bedford Road who had looked after him at her home during his illness. Matching the report with information on U-boat sinkings the vessel in question appears to have been the Greek ship *Vasilefs Georgios* on passage from Le Havre to Barry and sunk 3 miles NE of Pendeen.

The St. Ives Times had in the past drawn attention to the need for some sort of hospital facility in the town and the matter was raised again by a letter to the *Western Morning News* and reprinted in *The St. Ives Times* on September 6th 1918 in which the writer said:

> '. . . *Men of the mercantile marine are being brought in dying, broken, collapsed. This happens sufficiently often to make those who see them uncomfortable about our duty towards them. Whatever it is we have not done it. I am urged to write by what I have seen not half an hour ago, and the memory I have of other occasions. . . What would appear to be wanted is that a house should be taken immediately and adapted for the purpose of a small hospital with sufficient equipment and a small trained staff. Here these victims could die without having to travel miles on improvised ambulances to the nearest hospital. Here their agony could be alleviated without a cruel delay; here they could be nursed back to life; a quicker process when it is done with medical knowledge at the earliest moment. Dying, suffering or exhausted, they would know they were amongst friends . . .*'

With scenes such as these, brought about by the actions of the U-boats, often within sight and sound of the shore, is it any wonder that anyone who might be in a position to help the enemy would be suspect?

The idea of a small hospital in the town was received with enthusiasm, with an immediate anonymous offer of £1000 to start if off, but ran up against the problem of whether it should be a temporary facility to meet an immediate need or something more permanent which would meet the needs of the town in future. It was pointed out by the Editor of *The St. Ives Times* that the shareholders of the Hain Steamship Company had voted £5,000 'some time ago' for the erection of a hospital in memory of the late Captain Edward Hain and while this would no doubt be proceeded with later, something was needed '. . . *so that we may be prepared for what may happen during the coming winter months. . .*' Fortunately within the next few weeks the need to cater for survivors from ships sunk by U-boats no longer existed and the effort could be concentrated on a hospital to meet the general needs of the town. In due course the Edward Hain hospital was provided and it is ironic that it is now under threat.

From 1914 to 1918 130 ships were sunk by U-boats between Land's End and Bude. Their gross tonnage was some 210,000, and the ships ranged from steamers of 8,000 tons to fishing smacks of 17 tons under sail. Most were in the 1,000 to 4,000 ton range. The majority were sunk by torpedoes, others by gunfire and scuttling charges put on board by U-boat crews, and a few by mines which would have been laid by U-boats. Pendeen, St. Ives, Godrevy and Trevose were the areas where most activity took place, with the sinking of 110 out of the 130.

It was not all one-sided of course. Of the 390 U-boats built by Germany in WW1, 178 were sunk in action with the loss of some 5,300 officers and men, nearly 40% of the establishment. Most were sunk in the North Sea, the Channel and the Western Approaches, and we know of two sunk off the Scillies, two off the Lizard and one off Lundy. I have heard of one sunk in the vicinity of Cot Valley and would welcome any information on this. Six U-boats crossed the Atlantic to attack shipping off the U.S. eastern seaboard, sinking 91 vessels without loss to themselves.

The escalation of sinkings off the north Cornish coast in 1917 and the arrival of the Lawrences at Zennor may well have been thought of as more than co-inci-dence but the surge of activity was due to a decision by the German Navy rather than any help which might be expected from the Lawrences. There was a shortage of boats in 1915, those available being mostly on station in the North Sea. In 1916 the repercussions of the sinking of the *Lusitania* were still being felt and U-boat attacks were scaled down for fear of American reprisals but in February 1917 Germany declared unrestricted U-boat warfare. Boats were sent out from their bases for three or four weeks at a time to sink ships wherever they could find them and the western coasts of Britain, particularly north Cornwall, provided plenty of opportunities.

The first sinkings in 1915 were all in the Trevose area. The first was on 27th March when the *Vosges* on passage from Bordeaux to Liverpool was sunk by gunfire off Trevose Head by U-28. The last of the seven was sunk on 26th December 1915. One distressing incident was the sinking 20 miles west of Trevose Head of the *Armenian*, 8825 tons, bound for Avonmouth from Newport News, USA. Nine of her crew and 20 cattle attendants were killed and another 14 wounded. The ship was carrying general cargo and 3,000 mules for the army in France.

The lull in 1916 gave way to savage attacks in 1917 following the declaration of unrestricted submarine warfare. During 1917 the number of U-boats operating in the Trevose-Pendeen sector increased. Nine were identified, but 35 ships were sunk by submarines which were not identified. The 30th January 1917 was a day to remember. Ten small sailing smacks were captured off Trevose Head by an unidentified U-boat or boats and were sunk by gunfire or scuttling charges. A week later on the 8th February the St. Ives lugger *Mary Ann* was scuttled by a U-boat crew some 18 miles NNE of St. Ives Head. Mr. Matthew Stevens Snr and his crew were allowed to get into their punt and abandoned but were eventually picked up by a passing steamer the *Sheerness*. In appreciation the replacement vessel was named *Sheerness* and became a familiar part of the harbour scene. In 1918 the number of U-boats identified as operating between Trevose and Pendeen rose to 24 and there were probably others, which were not identified.

One submarine of particular interest to St. Ives was U-60. She was launched on 5th July 1916 and commissioned four months later. In January 1917 under Kapitänleutnant Schuster's command she came down through the Dover Straits and operated between the Scilly Isles and the southwest of Ireland, sinking several ships before returning home via the Orkneys at the end of February. Another tour of duty for Capt. Schuster commenced on 26th March, this time outward via the Orkneys to the southwest of Ireland and is marked by an example of the chivalry of some seafarers, even in wartime. On the 28th March in the North Sea they stopped the Danish barque *Thekla* but allowed her to proceed as she had faulty lifeboats. On that trip they again sank several vessels but because of bad weather could not use their weapons on 11 days, and they returned home via the Shetlands.

In February 1918 U-60 was placed under the command of Capt. Grünert. His first tour of duty started on 10th February when they left Kiel and travelled via the

Orkneys, Western Hebrides, the North Channel of the Irish Sea and the Bristol Channel down to the north coast of Cornwall. They sank four ships between Trevose and St. George's Channel and returned home on 12th March. The tour of duty which interests us started on 16th April, again under Capt. Grünert, around the north of Scotland to the north coast of Cornwall which was to be his main hunting ground. On 28th April they sank a ship off Morwenstow and on the evening of the 29th sank the French-owned ship *Saint Chamond* off St. Ives. The following day U-60 had an inconclusive encounter with a ship off Hartland Point and on 2nd May sank a ship off Bude before returning home again via the Orkneys. Capt Grünert in his report commended his Engineering Officer and the whole operation was praised by the German Fleet Commander.

Capt. Grünert paid another visit to the coast of Cornwall in July 1918 when he succeeded in sinking three ships before returning home in August. On this trip he appears to have had mechanical problems and he again praised the work of the Engineer and technicians. The last operational voyage set out from Kiel on 5th October heading for Biscaya in northern Spain, but hardly had the boat arrived in the area of action when orders came to return, and they arrived back in Kiel on 14th November. Having survived the war U-60 surrendered on 21st November 1918 and ignominiously ran aground on the east coast of England while on passage to the breaker's yard.

Saint Chamond's encounter with U-60 was not her first experience of the war at sea. On 3rd September 1915 while on passage from Rouen to Newcastle in ballast she was damaged when she struck a mine and was towed to Harwich for repairs. On 29th September 1917 she picked up survivors from the *Kildonan,* sunk two miles NNW of Pendeen lighthouse and later transferred them to a patrol vessel, which landed them at Penzance.

The *Saint Chamond* wreck lies about a mile and a half off Clodgy Point where she sank while an attempt was made to beach her. There are still St. Ives residents who remember the sinking, and one lady in particular, Mrs. Davies, widow of Kit Davies and now living at Truro, recalls how she joined half the town to watch the sinking from near the gas works, with the other half on the Island. Her son John also recalls his father telling him how he heard a tremendous explosion and ran all the way down Fore Street and the Digey to join crowds of people at Porthmeor to see the ship sink, going down stern first, leaving the bow straight up before finally sinking. Curiously we have no information as to casualties or the fate of the crew.

The ship, 2866 gross tons, built by Sir William Gray in his yard at West Hartlepool was launched in March 1913 and registered in the port of Nantes by her French owners Soc. Anon. des Chargeurs de l'Ouest. She was a typical example of cargo vessels built in the North East at that time and her 'particulars' as Ship No. 821 in the records of the Gray shipyard give an example of how a healthy order book in the yard provided employment for many other workers in the region. The triple expansion engines came from Gray's Central Marine Engine Works, the winches from Lynn of Sunderland, stockless anchors from Byers of Sunderland and windlass from Emerson Walker of Gateshead.

The ship's manifest is not available, but she was on passage from Glasgow to St. Nazaire carrying railway locomotives and other railway material. The Springburn district of Glasgow had been renowned as a centre for locomotive building since 1831, and in 1903 the various concerns amalgamated to form the North British Locomotive Company, familiarly known as the NB. From information in the records of the NB Company, kindly supplied by the Mitchell Library, it is fairly certain that the locomotives were built by them and were destined for the French State Railways. The NB Company built locomotives for railways all over the world, ranging from 15 ton tank engines for the Darjeeling Himalayan Railway to machines of 100 tons or more for other railways in India and South Africa. They were transported from the works on huge trailers hauled by traction engines, and crowds would gather to see them being manoeuvred through the city streets on their way to the docks with a precision born of years of experience.

In the First World War 695 NB engines went to the war zones, and five of them are probably those on the seabed off Clodgy Point. What is particularly interesting is that these five locomotives appear to have been a replacement order for five out of an earlier batch of 40 destined for French State Railways which were '. . . lost in transit . . .'. They could hardly have been mislaid and the assumption is that they also were lost at sea.

The wreck is well-known to local fishermen, divers and members of sub-aqua clubs. Mr. Phil Austin, an Instructor with the British Sub-Aqua Club regularly dives on the wreck and he has confirmed for me that five large locomotives lie scattered around the remains of the ship, together with a vast quantity of locomotive boiler tubes and track components. There are no tenders, so the assumption is that they were delivered as part of the earlier batch of 40 and were sitting in a depot in France awaiting replacement locomotives. The ship's gun has been recovered and now has pride of place at the entrance of Mr. Richard Larn's Maritime Heritage Centre at Charlestown.

Having talked about U-boats and sunken ships we are at the moment no nearer to establishing the official reason for the exclusion of Lawrence and his wife. A preliminary search of likely War Office and Foreign Office sources has revealed nothing so far, but the search will continue. In the meantime all I can suggest is that we leave it with Lawrence's friend Lady Cynthia Asquith who wrote in her diary for Tuesday 16th October 1917 that Lawrence had visited her to tell her of the events at Higher Tregerthen. She said: '. . . *I promised to do what I could in the matter, but doubt whether it will be much - after all, the woman is a German and it doesn't seem unreasonable . . .'. (Lady Cynthia Asquith: Diaries 1915-1918. Hutchinson of London, 1968*).

It may be of interest to readers to know something of the sources used for research into the maritime aspects of this article. The initial source was the Courtney Library and Cornish History Archive at Truro, still, unfortunately a research centre unknown to many people. Owned and managed by the Royal Institution of Cornwall it is a private library for the use of members, but non-members are welcome and may have access for research free of charge: a donation to the Library's Book Fund would be appreciated from visitors who benefit from its facilities. It is the oldest established Cornish history research centre in the County and in addition to the maritime subjects it has an extensive range of records on many aspects of Cornish history and its people, including photographs. One of the main sources I found of use was volume 1 of the Larn Shipwreck Index, by Richard and Bridget Larn, a mine of information. Details of the Library and its facilities, also a leaflet dealing specifically with sources for maritime research are available from the Librarian, The Royal Institution of Cornwall, River Street, Truro, TR1 2SJ.

The other source, of magnificent proportions, was the Library of the Maritime Information Centre at the National Maritime Museum at Greenwich. This houses what may well be the best collection of primary source material on maritime subjects anywhere, including original documents, journals, log-books etc. The Centre updates the collections through computer technology, which helps those who wish to carry out their own research at Greenwich, and enables the Museum to respond more quickly and effectively to enquiries.

Five of these Express Passenger 'Compound' locomotives were built in Glasgow by the North British Locomotive Co. in 1917/18 for the French State Railways. It is likely that they were the five carried by S.S. Saint Chamond *and which now lie on the seabed off Clodgy Point.*

MOLTENO PLACE & the SOUTH AFRICA CONNECTION

Suggestions last year that Heathrow Airport and Kensington Gardens should be renamed made me think of how towns, streets, buildings and public gardens acquired their names in the first place. The origins of some of the street names in St. Ives are lost in the mists of antiquity, others have been given by the Town Council in association with housing schemes. Some bear the names of individuals — Wesley Place, Harry's Court, Dick's Hill, for example. Bunker's Hill probably commemorates a British victory at Bunker Hill in the American War of Independence. The Crimean war is commemorated in Alma Terrace and the Malakoff. The Malakoff was a strongly fortified hill in the defences of Sebastopol and the scene of some of the fiercest fighting in the campaign between British, French and Russian troops. The Malakoff in St. Ives is said to have been given the name when it was just a rocky outcrop and local lads were seen attacking and defending it with sticks in mock battle. The likely origins of street names in the town have been the subject of letters and articles in St. Ives newspapers for the past hundred years. Cyril Noall had a go at some of them in the 1960's, and more recently the origins of the Digey and Virgin Street were discussed in an article in *The St. Ives Times & Echo* on 14th January 1991.

One name that has always intrigued me is Molteno Place in the Stennack. Like the house name *Manzanita,* named after an exotic shrub common in the mid-west of the U.S.A., it had a foreign flavour. I imagined it to have been brought back by a St. Ives emigrant and perhaps named after a gold mine in Australia or California, or a diamond mine in South Africa. It was only recently, however, that I was privileged to discover its origin from the one person in town in a position to know the story — Captain John Kemp MBE — a few months before his recent death at 93 years of age. It is him we have to thank for adding to our local knowledge in respect of Molteno Place.

When Captain Kemp sailed with the Andrew Weir 'Bank' line in Glasgow as a

Master Mariner he was afforded the privilege of taking his wife with him on his voyages, a facility not permitted by the Hain Steamship Company with whom he previously served. On one occasion when his ship was in Cape Town and his wife Ann was with him they visited a locality which included the name Molteno, where his mother was born and spent much of her childhood.

Her parents had emigrated from St. Ives to South Africa where her father, William Shugg, worked as a builder. When the family returned to St. Ives in about 1870 Mr. Shugg bought a piece of land adjacent to Eden House and on it he built the terrace of three houses which we see today. He called it Molteno Place as a reminder of the time they spent in South Africa and the roundel bearing the name can still be seen on the gable end of the top house where the family lived.

In the course of time Captain Kemp's father married Mr. Shugg's daughter, and when Captain Kemp was a boy the Kemp family moved from the Wharf, where his father had a hairdressing salon, to the house in Molteno Place. He recalls the days when Mr. Phillips' stables were across the road and Miss Treweeke lived in Eden House. She had a pony and jingle and would ask Mrs. Kemp if young John could drive her up to Trencrom. Among his memories of living there is the day in 1912 when a young man came to the door to collect a parcel he was taking to Kemp relatives in America. Sadly neither the young man nor the parcel reached America. He was William Carbines, lost on the *Titanic*. His body was returned to St. Ives and he was buried in Barnoon cemetery.

We now know why the terrace in St. Ives was called Molteno Place, but what was the origin of the name Molteno in South Africa? In 1831 a young man of 17, John Charles Molteno, in due course to become Sir John Charles, set sail from England for South Africa. After a short spell in the South Africa Library he joined a business house and never looked back. He acquired a sheep-farm and despite the scepticism of other farmers achieved considerable success with Merino sheep. He then founded his own business dealing with Britain and the Far East, set up his own Bank and became very rich in the process.

In 1854, at the age of 40 he became a Member of the Legislative Assembly when the Cape Colony was granted Representative Government, and in 1872 when the Cape was given Responsible Government he became the first Prime Minister. His family were old-established back home in England from about 1730, and their name of Molteno is said to have come from Molteno near Milan in Northern Italy.

While gold and diamonds were being feverishly sought in other parts of the country the Eastern Cape had a different treasure — coal. The first railway in the Cape opened in 1864, and from then until the early 1870's the railways were at a great disadvantage as all coal had to be imported. In the early 1870's coal deposits were discovered in the Eastern Cape in the mountainous area north of Queens-town. A village was established there some 300 kilometres north-west of East

London in 1874 and because of its importance to the economy of the Province it was named Molteno after Sir John Charles Molteno, the Prime Minister. In addition there are thoroughfares called Molteno Road, Crescent etc, including a Molteno Reservoir, in towns in the Cape provinces. Molteno Place in St. Ives, therefore, has honourable credentials.

In a roundabout way Carbis Bay has an indirect connection with Sir John Molteno. One of his sons, Percy Alport Molteno, married Elizabeth Martin Currie, a daughter of Sir Donald Currie the shipping magnate. Percy became a Board Member of Sir Donald's 'Castle' later 'Union Castle' shipping lines for which Greville Ewing Matheson of Boskerris Vean was Publicity Manager for 40 years. It's a small world.

ST. IVES to CALIFORNIA in 1871
Sarah Glasson's Story

In 1871 Sarah Glasson, 10 years old, with her mother and sisters, left St. Ives to join her father in California. When Sarah was 90 she was persuaded by her family in California to record her memories and experiences of life in Cornwall and California, and a copy of her memoirs was sent to relatives in St. Ives some 50 years ago. The document lay dormant until recently when a St. Ives descendant sent me a copy as being possible material for a feature in *The St. Ives Times & Echo*. The memoir is too long for inclusion here, but copies have been lodged with the St. Ives Trust Archive Study Centre and the Sears Historical Museum in Grass Valley, California. This commentary enlarges on aspects of Sarah's experiences and the Glasson family in California.

The emigration of the Glasson family to America in 1871 followed a pattern familiar to thousands of Cornish families. Father would go on ahead to a pre-arranged job, or perhaps to an area where Cornish families had settled and there was a prospect of work, and having secured employment and prepared a home he would then send for the rest of the family.

The Glassons in West Cornwall were noted for the number of blacksmiths they produced and Sarah talks of her father Josiah Glasson who was a blacksmith in St. Ives. Her mother, Sarah, was one of a large Craze family, one of whom William, was subsequently Mayor of St. Ives. The family home and the blacksmith's shop were in the Stennack and after Josiah left St. Ives for California in 1867 the family moved to a house on Tregenna farm where they spent four happy years. Sarah mentions some of the books she read including Thomas à Kempis. How many children today, at ten, would read him for pleasure!

Josiah found employment as a blacksmith with the principal mining company in North Bloomfield, a town of some 1700 inhabitants, which grew up around mining operations dating from around the 1850's, situated about 12 miles from Nevada City. The company worked the Malakoff North Bloomfield mine, the world's largest hydraulic operation. In 1871 he had decided to return to St. Ives but had gone only a few miles when he was persuaded to return by the Company's Chief Engineer and Superintendent who asked him to take charge of all the mine blacksmiths in connection with a major project at North Bloomfield. The hydraulic mining operation, which replaced the pick and shovel and the gold pan, used powerful water

Josiah Glasson

monitors similar to those used for china clay extraction in Cornwall. These required vast amounts of water and the means of disposing of the tons of waste gravel, mud and water from the mining operations. The project on which Josiah was employed was a great mining engineering feat — the making of an 8,000 feet long drainage tunnel through solid rock.

On accepting the job Josiah immediately sent for his family in St. Ives. It says much for the marriage bonds and the family ties that on receipt of a letter from

America enclosing a bankers' draft to pay the fare a family would up-sticks and be on their way. Sarah pays tribute to her mother who had never been outside St. Ives. Mrs. Glasson however, may well have known something of what to expect in California through letters from her husband. It was certainly the case that many families in West Cornwall could tell you more about people and what was happening in, say, Butte, Montana than they could about what was happening in Truro.

Sarah dismissed the journey from St. Ives to California in two short paragraphs, but it could not have been easy for a mother with four young children. First of all by carriage to Hayle, then by ship to Bristol for an overnight stop. Next day by train to Liverpool to join ship for a two-week rough crossing of the Atlantic, followed by a two-week train journey from New York to Colfax and finally a buggy ride to Grass Valley, where they lived for a period before moving to a company house at North Bloomfield.

Sarah became a teacher and her experience makes an interesting comparison with present day arrangements. Her school teacher and her father thought she should be a teacher as she was '. . . a good speller . . .' although she herself was not keen, and she tells how at 18 she took the teacher's examination in Nevada City and was granted a second grade. With this simple qualification, no experience and no teacher training she applied for a single-handed school and was immediately appointed. After early disappointment with parent problems she proved herself an able teacher. She later married and with her husband ran a prosperous meat market business.

The narrative shows that emigration to America was not necessarily an escape from the economic troubles in Cornwall in the late 1800's. In Josiah's time as a mine blacksmith in North Bloomfield we have an example of how one mining technique was overtaken by another, eventually leading to its own demise and the collapse of a community. The hydraulic mines, by washing down the mountain sides produced a vast amount of waste which was channelled into the Yuba and Sacramento rivers, causing extensive environmental damage not only to the rivers but also the surrounding farmlands, the silt even reaching as far as San Francisco and out into the Pacific Ocean through the Golden Gate. The farmers fought the mining company and won their case, the first of its kind in the U.S.A. and the hydraulic mines were forced to close. Families had to leave, resulting in the collapse of local businesses and almost overnight North Bloomfield became a ghost town. Sarah and her husband had to sell what was left of their business at a knock-down price and move away, relying on their children for support.

The towns of Grass Valley and Nevada City survived and are now desirable residential locations, generating business from their historical mining connections. Through the concerted efforts of local citizens over several years the site of North Bloomfield and its principal mine, the Malakoff Mine, are now within the Malakoff Diggins State Historic Park, with picnic and camping grounds and rental cabins. Some of North Bloomfield's original buildings have survived. Others, including the school, have been reconstructed and a museum contains artefacts connected with the town's mining history.

Sarah's narrative is cut short with the words 'Not completed'. If Sarah had continued she would almost certainly have mentioned her father's brother John Glasson who left St. Ives in 1864 when he was 13. Perhaps he went out to join other Glasson family members and may have been put on a train at St. Erth like Richard Jose, the famous singer, who as a young lad, was put on a train at Camborne with a label attached to his jacket to join his uncle at a mining camp in Virginia City, Nevada.

From being a moulder in a Nevada City foundry John Glasson went on to become a prominent citizen with interests in local businesses in Nevada City and Grass Valley. He became Treasurer, Superintendent and a Director of the Nevada County Narrow Gauge Railway, which operated a branch line between Colfax on the Southern Pacific Railway main line and Grass Valley and Nevada City. He had his own food stores and in 1885 bought the Grass Valley Gas Co. Three years later he bought the Electric Light Co. and merged the two to form the Grass Valley Gas & Electric Co. of which he was President for several years before he sold out to a major organisation. He and his daughter Bernice made several visits to their relatives in North Terrace, St. Ives and he died in 1925 aged 73.

In a review of business interests in Grass Valley in 1895, the *Daily Morning Union* newspaper had this to say about progressive businessmen there:

> '. . . *It goes to show what push, energy and enterprise will accomplish. No better example of this can be shown in Grass Valley than by referring to John Glasson . . .*'

Bernice Glasson was much respected in Grass Valley and western Nevada County for her tireless work in community projects and charities, particularly the local hospital, and in 1956 she was voted Citizen of the Year. Her achievements and those of the Glasson family were acknowledged by the naming of Glasson Way near the hospital, and her commitment to local organisations was honoured during her lifetime and by the Grass Valley newspaper *The Union* when she died in September 1966.

Cornishmen who went to America took their musical talents with them and band and choral competitions were annual events in Grass Valley. A group known as John Farrell's Choir had its origins in the Grass Valley Methodist Church at about the time Josiah Glasson and his family went there, subsequently taking the name of The Grass Valley Carol Choir. They were noted for their expertise in rendering Cornish carols and sang in hospitals, on the streets and in the State capital Sacramento. They frequently performed over the radio and on one occasion sang from the 2,000 foot level of a mine in Grass Valley. So many men wanted to sing that another group formed the Merritt Carol Choir, joining forces with the Grass Valley singers on appropriate occasions.

It is not yet known if the Glasson brothers were members of the Grass Valley Carol Choir, but John Glasson was certainly musically talented. He married into a French family and his wife, Marie Rose Montes, was an accomplished musician and composer. In his book *The French Connection, The French in Nevada County, California,* Michel Janicot tells how in the Glasson home on West Main Street, Grass Valley (which still survives) '. . . *her salon was the city's most influential center where prominent citizens gathered to discuss new ideas and current political events . . .*', and in the Nevada County Historical Society newsletter of June 1966 Sybil L. Leuteneker tells how in the Glasson home there was an expensive organ and the silk lambrequins which adorned the windows of the parlor (*sic*) were imported from France. John, Marie Rose and their daughter Bernice, all sang in the senior choir of St. Patrick's Catholic Church in Grass Valley, and in 1921 the local newspaper reported that at the Christmas masses the soloist was Mrs. John Glasson (soprano), supported by daughter Bernice also a soprano, and husband John, tenor.

West Cornwall voices were again heard in Grass Valley with a St. Ives' voice among them as 49 of the 72 members of the Mousehole Male Voice Choir, the second oldest in Cornwall and celebrating its 90th anniversary this year (1999), together with a group of supporters, spent eleven days in the Grass Valley area and three in San Francisco.

My research discovered Glasson descendants in Grass Valley and Sacramento, and a happy outcome of our research has been that they and my St. Ives friend are now in touch, restoring family links between Cornwall and California which have been missing for some 40 years. A bonus is that among the enquiries I also have found a Glasson cousin and family in Sacramento. They have subsequently visited St Ives and we have established a happy relationship.

HANDS ACROSS the SEA
St. Ives, Cornwall & St. Ives, New South Wales

My old school atlas shows large areas of the Earth's surface coloured red, indicating countries which made up the British Empire. The red has gone from the atlases which my grandchildren now use, as the Empire is consigned to history and a proposed Museum of Empire in Bristol. The most recent Commonwealth Conference provided further evidence of the loosening of the ties with the mother country, and Australia is on the way to cutting loose and becoming a Republic. Things were very different in 1908 when the Empire was a potent force and Queen Victoria's reign was still very much in people's minds.

In August 1908 Mr John Pearce, Mayor of St. Ives wrote to the Editor of the *Weekly Summary* enclosing a letter from Mr E. W. Smethurst, Secretary of the British Empire League in Sydney, New South Wales in which he said:

> '. . . *For the purpose of promoting a feeling of kinship amongst the children of the Empire, we are providing for an exchange of Empire flags and especially between places bearing the same names, so that flying over schools on high days they may remind the children of their cousins over the sea . . .*'

The League had already sent a flag from Launceston, Tasmania to Launceston in Cornwall, and they proposed a similar exchange between St. Ives in New South Wales and St. Ives Cornwall.

The writer indicated that the schoolchildren of St. Ives, New South Wales wish to claim kinship with those in St. Ives Cornwall and for that purpose were sending a Union flag 12ft by 6ft with the inscription *From the children of St. Ives, New South Wales to those of St. Ives Cornwall 1908*. It was their hope that scholars would open correspondence with each other and that if a photograph of the town could be sent it would be framed and placed in the school there as a constant reminder of the kinsfolk at home.

Accompanying this letter was one from William A Crawford, a teacher at the school in New South Wales, in which he said:

> '. . . *The children of St. Ives Public School are delighted to be able to send a flag home to St. Ives, England. Our little village received its name at the suggestion and*

request of three Cornishmen who settled here in their early days when thinking of their home over the seas. Our St. Ives is a beautiful little village about 11 miles from Sydney on the North Shore railway line and nestles quietly amongst orchards of oranges, lemons and other fruits. The air is pure, bracing and healthy and invigorating and the people are naturally happy and contented'.

On receipt of the flag the Mayor called a meeting of the teachers and managers of the National and Council schools at which it was agreed the flag would be held by each school, year and year about, with the Council School having the first year's ownership and that a flag would be sent to New South Wales together with views of St. Ives and appropriate expressions of appreciation, courtesy and loyalty on behalf of the children of St. Ives.

The New South Wales flag was first raised at the Stennack School on Empire Day 1909 with suitable speeches and celebrations, the ceremony being attended by 1229 children of whom 741 were from the Council Schools, 271 from the National School, 147 from Island Road and 70 from Halsetown. Each child received a bun and a medal specially struck for the occasion, which was worn with a tricolour ribbon. It was very much a 'Flag Day' in the town as in addition to the New South Wales flag, the Town Flag flew from the Malakoff, the flag presented by Sir Thomas Lipton flew over the Shamrock Lodge, while others flew from the Drill Hall, the National School and several business places and private residences.

In 1939 another flag was received from New South Wales with greetings for the tercentenary of the granting of the town Charter in 1639. This also was a 12ft by 6ft Union flag and flew bravely on a special pole on the Island where it was raised by the Mayoress, Mrs C W Curnow, as part of the Charter Week celebration. Apart from recording the initial meetings and decisions regarding the 1908 flag the school logbooks are strangely silent as to any subsequent occasions on which the flag was flown or any follow-up of the proposed links between schools and the children themselves.

Some special importance must have been attached in Australia to the raising of the flag from Cornwall as it was unfurled in December 1909 at St. Ives New South Wales by no less a personage than the wife of the Premier — Mrs Wade — and it was reported that at the ceremony, in response to an enquiry as to the origin of the name of the village a lady had come forward to say that her son, a Mr. Nancarrow, a Cornishman, had given it the name St. Ives. So far I have not discovered if he had St. Ives connections. There must have been some communications between the two towns as at the hoisting of the flag in August 1939 Mr Bastian, Headmaster of the Boys School, mentioned that the flag sent to Australia in 1908 was hoisted at the New South Wales school on their Jubilee Day, May 27th, while the message from New South Wales trusted '. . . that the bonds may be ever closer drawn . . .'. It is also unlikely that the New South Wales School would have been aware of the forthcoming Charter celebrations unless someone in St. Ives had told them.

Whether our flag exists in New South Wales is a matter for inquiry. Their 1908 flag to us appears to have been lost but the 1939 flag is held at the Junior School, Trenwith Burrows. The school also has a medal and photographs of the 1909 ceremony and no doubt there are other medals in existence among family treasures in the town. Taking photographs of 1229 children in groups must have been an exhausting undertaking and the *Weekly Summary* reported overhearing one impatient youngster saying: 'Oh my gosh! They'll never be tooken for generations'. A photograph of the 1939 flag appeared in *The Times and Echo* on November 12th1993 on the occasion of a visit to the school by Reverend Allan Lanham and his wife who live in Jimboomba, Queensland, and whose Church bears the name St. Ives and is twinned with St Ives Wesley.

I have known of the flag affair for some time and have been interested in trying to find out more about the 1908 contacts — whether any letters survive, why Mr Nancarrow and his companions decided to settle at that particular place and even perhaps consider the possibility of renewal of the 1908 links. To establish a village the early settlers presumably had families and it is possible that they had St. Ives, Cornwall connections. The opportunity to find out came a few months ago when a friend who lives in Sydney called on me while on a business visit to Bristol. He was interested to hear of the exchange and being familiar with both St Ives locations he offered to make inquiries on his return to Sydney. At the same time I asked Mr Peter Gleeson, Headteacher at the Junior School, if he and his staff would be interested in trying to restore the links with Australia. The reaction was positive and enthusiastic as such a move would offer opportunities for the exchange of projects between the pupils, accompanied by the gift of a Cornish flag.

The enquiries in New South Wales have borne fruit in the form of a response from Mr. Ray Daley, Principal of the St. Ives South Primary School, who also is enthusiastic about the prospect of establishing a relationship with us. The school with which the flags were exchanged — St. Ives Central Primary — was closed about five years ago. From being a little village in 1908 St. Ives is now part of the suburbs of Sydney, with two primary schools and a high school. Of these St. Ives South Primary, which is in the process of changing its name to St. Ives Primary and has links with the High School, is considered the most appropriate. Mr. Daley has already sent some interesting items connected with his school. Among these are the school information book which includes the dates of school holidays from now until the year 2000; a silver spoon issued in 1988 to commemorate the 20th anniversary of the founding of the school, badges for captain, vice-captain and librarian, also banners and certificates for scholastic achievement. These have been passed to Mr. Gleeson who will follow up the school connection. I hope to find out more about the Cornish origins and we also hope that projects will be developed enabling pupils here and in St. Ives, New South Wales to find out more about their respective lifestyles and the history of their towns. The prospects are exciting, not only for historical research but also links between children which may develop into lifetime friendships and, who knows, there may also be scope for wider civic liaison on such things as tourism. Progress will be reported and it is hoped that as the relationship between the two schools develops the children themselves will be encouraged to use their computing skills and their personal experiences to produce contributions to *The Times and Echo* and its opposite number in St. Ives, New South Wales.

The St. Ives Weekly Summary in May 1909 reported that on Empire Day at Sennen two visitors obtained a couple of masts from a fisherman, rigged a flagstaff and soon had the Union Jack flying from the top. After firing six volleys with their revolvers they gave three cheers for the King, while a gramophone played the *Empire March*.

When we get to the stage of flying the flag from New South Wales over St. Ives Junior School on high days, the celebrations will be a little more restrained but no less enthusiastic although we may not be able to get the Prime Minister's wife to hoist the flag.

IT PAYS to ADVERTISE

Between 1889 and 1910 James Uren White, Editor of the *St. Ives Weekly Summary* newspaper, regularly inserted jingles advertising his paper. With the transition to the *St. Ives Times* the tradition was continued by Martin Cock, one of my favourites being his collection of *That's* which included — *'Tennyson could take a sheet of paper; write a poem on it worth £1,300.* — That's Genius. *Rothschild can write a few words on paper and make it worth £1,000,000.* — That's Capital. *A man can run a business and not advertise.* — That's Foolishness. *A large number of people advertise in the St. Ives Times.* — That's Common Sense'.

Advertisements are an important source of revenue for a newspaper, particularly a local paper relying on local firms for its business, and the level of advertising can reflect the state of business in the town. With the closing down of long-established firms in St. Ives and the moves towards out-of-town supermarkets, there are many goods and services which are no longer on offer in the town, and it is of interest to have a look at what was being advertised in the past. Picking a date at random, I have had a look at the *St. Ives Times* for July 1st 1921, in which approximately three quarters of the available space was devoted to advertisements.

One of the striking things about the July 1921 issue is the range of goods and services on offer — it seems that there was little need to go elsewhere for almost anything. Traders also geared their stock to meet current situations. Following the coal strikes of October 1920 and May 1921, documented by Eddie Murt in his book *Downlong Days,* there was a great shortage of coal in the town, and Lanham's, normally associated with art materials and wines and spirits, took advantage of the situation by advertising on the front page the laying in of large stocks of peat, for which they offered quotations for 25 to 1,000 blocks with free delivery. Coal merchants may also have laid in stocks of alternative fuels, but if so they didn't advertise it.

In 1921 there was a far greater choice of grocery shops than we have at present and several were regular advertisers. The Star Tea Company at 18 Fore Street encouraged people to save coal by buying cooked foods such as their 'tinned and glass tongues, tinned mutton' etc as well as offering fresh slab Genoa, Madeira and Seed cake at reduced prices. Mr. Hine, whose grocery business was also in Fore

THE NEW CABINET FOR TESTING THE COOLING PROPERTIES
OF MITRE FRUIT DRINKS

A brilliant invention no doubt, but the cooling properties of Mitre Fruit
Drinks can be easily proved without the aid of any special apparatus.

MITRE FRUIT DRINKS
PURE · HEALTHFUL · REFRESHING

	per bottle
LIME JUICE CORDIAL	10d & 1/2
LEMON BARLEY WATER	
LEMON SQUASH (Clear or Cloudy)	11d & 1/4
GRAPE FRUIT SQUASH	
ORANGE SQUASH	1/- & 1/8

*KIA-ORA, ROSE'S, STOWER'S and other makes
also kept in Stock.*

INTERNATIONAL STORES
The Greatest Grocers in the World
CEYLINDO TEA

Street, offered a range of Cornish specialities — butter, cheese, cream cheese and bacon, with delivery in all parts of the District. Where now can one get Cornish bacon? Mr. Herbert and his son at Chy-an-Chy extended their grocery business by advertising as 'General Store Dealers', including an Agency for Peacock's Sanitary Paints. Mrs. T. Quick in Tregenna Place offering her good selection of groceries, confectionery etc also solicited '. . . *a share of your patronage . . .*'.

Fore Street, of course, had those hardy standbys Simpsons and Comley's. Simpsons, in addition to offering '. . . *the most up-to-date ideas in men's outfitting in town . . .,*' were also agents for Union Castle Line to South Africa, White Star and Principal Lines to America and Canada, and Orient Line to Australia. How many St. Ives people, I wonder, setting off for a new life, bought their steamer tickets across the mahogany counter in Simpsons? Mr. Comley's advertisement for summer footwear was graced by a charming motif. It may well represent a flower, but looks a little like a lady in a bikini.

Cryséde carried a large advertisement announcing the move from temporary premises opposite Digey Corner to new premises in the lower part of Lanham's shop in High Street, formerly used as the Fancy and Stationery Department. We usually associate Cryséde with elegant dresses for ladies, but in this advertisement they were aiming at the younger generation — *'Most kiddies love beautiful and bright colours instinctively, and will take care of and love a frock made of any of our beautiful fabrics. Our silk and crepe-de-chine is of pre-war price and superfine quality, while the colours and designs are genuine works of art. Wash these how much you will, they retain their colour and beauty'.* Who now advertises T-shirts and jeans with such style?

Mr. Leddra, M.P.S., was not satisfied with one advertisement — he had two. One, with a large staring eye, gave details of eye-testing, spectacle fitting and repairs, the other extolled the virtues of Jonteel face powder '. . . *Acceptable to the*

Mr Charlie Peters, his wife Irene and nephew Michael, in their well-stocked shop at 52 Fore Street, St. Ives in 1962. In addition to the extensive range of cigarettes and sweets they also sold a selection of fruit and vegetables.

most sensitive skin. Delightfully fragrant, perfumed with Jonteel, the costly new odor (sic) of 26 flowers . . .'. Mr. Winsor announced the removal of his dental surgery to premises above W.H. Smith's in Street-an-Pol, with attendance on Tuesdays and Fridays. Ladies could also make an appointment with Miss J. Wade the resident Corsetiere for Spirella Corsets, at Primrose Cottage.

There is probably little demand these days for horse-shoeing in the town, but then Mr. John Ninnis offered this service at his forge opposite the Wesleyan Church. He also did boat work and made wrought iron gates and railings to order, while Cornish ranges were a speciality. Mr. Alfred H. Cock also offered his services as general smith and range maker at his premises on the Wharf and at the same time advertised for an apprentice. J. Luke and Son who worked as smiths and fitters on the Wharf dealing with ranges and lawn mowers, wanted an apprentice to the smithing. When I needed a replacement part a little while ago for a Rayburn stove I was lucky to find what I needed at Liskeard!

Mr. William Henry Care offered 2-pint aluminium kettles for 5s.6d. with reductions for cash at his shop in Gabriel Street opposite the Free Library. You could also get your gramophone repaired and a new tyre put on a perambulator wheel at the Dove Street workshop of Mr. W. Corin, motor and cycle fitter. There

was no shortage of choice when it came to builders, decorators, plumbers and chimney sweeps.

Entertainment in the town was well advertised. The Pavilion at Porthminster beach offered a 'Fun Night', with the exhortation *'Come in your thousands'*. The Cinema, at the bottom of Barnoon Hill, built about ten years earlier as a 'place of amusement', later to become the Palais de Danse, and then the studio of the late Dame Barbara Hepworth, had a large advertisement with details of the two programmes for the week. These consisted of a main film, a supporting film, a comedy and news in pictorial form. There was also a synopsis of the various films for each of the programmes. In this particular week one film, *The Best of Luck*, listed as '. . . *The tremendous Drury Lane melodrama of daring deeds, high romance and startling surprises . . .'* included the following:

'. . . *The pursuit of a woman riding a motorcycle, by a band of ruffians in a high powered car that plunges over a cliff into an abyss; a search for treasure on a sunken galleon in a submarine; a hand to hand fight with axes between two men in diving suits, five fathoms under the sea. Neither time nor expense were spared to make this production more magnificent, more compelling, more excitingly astonishing than the original stage production which took London by storm . . .'*

No, it wasn't a James Bond original, and I wonder how a fight with axes between two men in diving suits five fathoms beneath the sea was produced on the London stage. You had to see the film to find out who had *The Best of Luck* — my guess is that it was one of the men in a diving suit and the woman on the motorbike.

The Cinema was up-to-date with its choice of films. A couple picked at random were *Madame Peacock* featuring Nazimova, Metro's biggest moneymaking star, and *Daddy Long Legs* with Mary Pickford.

For those who sought more sedate pleasures Payne & Son begged to inform their patrons and the public generally that their picnic grounds at Carbis Bay were open. Their telephone number incidentally was 1 x 4. Can anyone explain this? Carbis Bay was a popular venue for picnics as J. Williams also advertised his Carbis Valley picnic grounds, close to the beach, established 1849. For those who preferred a walk in the country, clotted cream teas could be obtained at Trencrom Cottage, Lelant, where E. Hocking offered the best and cheapest for the money.

For those who preferred to ride rather than walk Warren & Ninnes offered Char-a-Banc tours from their garage in St. Andrew's Street. No details were given but quotations would be given on request. Mr. Blewett, with his familiar Crimson Tours, was more forthcoming, with details of dates, places and fares. At that time his garage was at Hayle, but bookings could be made at Mr. Welch's, Tregenna Hill, Mrs. Cowling, Grocer, Carbis Bay, and Mr. Sandow, Grocer, Lelant.

The regular trips were usually in and around West Penwith, but special trips to places like Fowey and Tintagel would be arranged in the season. Mr. John Uren Phillips also offered trips from his Livery Stables in Bullans Lane at fares cheaper than Mr. Blewett's, as well as offering Jersey cars and Carriages of all descriptions on hire.

Education and self-improvement were not neglected. Mr. Ernest White received pupils for the piano and singing at 2 Fore Street, while Mr. Trevor White, Professor of Music, received pupils for pianoforte, violin, mandoline, and voice production, singing theory and harmony, at The Gew, Street-an-Pol. Miss Shakerley advertised her St. Eia's School, which took boarders and day pupils, and Mr. Wagner, Head Master of the Grammar School at Hayle offered successful preparation for commercial life, or for professional or other examinations.

Two areas in which newspaper advertising now has blossomed as against 1921 are property sales and eating out. Estate Agents' notices now account for a large share of the advertising space, but in July 1921 property advertising was minimal. There were no photographs and no Estate Agent descriptions of the few houses involved. There were no holiday homes and definitely no tiled shower rooms. Mr. John Saundry, House and Estate Agent, had a regular space on the back page as well as a four-line entry in the 'small ads' indicating that he had been favoured with instructions to let some excellent furnished houses. Lanham's offered a house in Primrose Valley to let unfurnished; one in West Place was offered for sale by a Solicitor in Penzance, and a handful, all in the 'small ads,' were offered by private individuals. Many deals were done by word of mouth and a hand-shake. I recall being told of my grandfather's sister, Mrs. Janie Trevorrow, going up the street to the shops and coming back to say that she had bought a house while she was there. Advertising of eating out in those days was confined to cream teas at Trencrom Cottage, the picnic grounds at Carbis Bay and Mr. Charles W. Curnow's Restaurant in Tregenna Place.

The town still has many good businesses and services to offer, but the 1921 level of advertising indicates that the range of choice has been reduced from what was on offer to our parents and grandparents. The lesson is to advertise what is available, for, as James Uren White said: '. . . *Trying to do business without advertising is like winking in the dark; you may know what you are doing, but nobody else does . . .*'

ST. IVES ARTILLERY VOLUNTEERS
& the DRUM MAJOR

The St. Ives Artillery Volunteers Memorial

The recent temporary removal of the memorial to the St. Ives Artillery Volunteers from the west wall of the Trenwith aisle in St. Ives Parish Church for cleaning and restoration, gives us the opportunity of looking at the background to the unit. In 1779 Great Britain had its hands full with the rebellion of the Colonists in north-east America, leading to the American War of Independence. The heavy calls on the Navy, protecting ships carrying men and war supplies across the Atlantic depleted the cover of the Western Approaches and the English Channel, which in turn gave our enemies in Europe — France, Spain and Holland — an opportunity of attempting to seize command of the Channel. A fleet of some 60-odd vessels, with 50,000 men and 400 transports was assembled at ports in north west Spain and in August 1779 set out with the intention of attempting a landing near Plymouth. They got part way up the Channel but an easterly gale blew them out again and the immediate danger was over.

The incident, however, caused alarm and a review of the coastal defences which were found to be in a poor or non-existing state. Plans were made to provide batteries at strategic locations round the coast and the men to man them were provided by County militia or volunteers. For at least three centuries St. Ives had some form of military protection. The Borough Accounts for 1701/2 record payments to gunners as well as bell ringers to celebrate the return of King William from Holland. In 1705/6 1s.6d. was paid '. . . *to put the gun and carriages to the Island . . .*' In 1708 the accounts included 2s.0d. paid in drink to the gunners, and in 1781 John Knill was in command of a Corps of Volunteers.

As a busy seaport the security of shipping using St. Ives was of major concern, and a threat of invasion by Napoleon's forces resulted in a strengthening of the town's defences with the setting up of a Voluntary Infantry Regiment commanded by Lieut-Colonel James Halse, whose name is perpetuated in the village of Halsetown. My family had a tenuous link with the Napoleonic period through the nickname 'Boney'. The story handed down is that at the time when the threat of invasion was real the town was alarmed by a report that a group of men with pikes was seen approaching the town from the western hills and that 'Boney and his army were on the way'. It turned out to be a Richards ancestor from Zennor with his many sons and their pitchforks coming to help a relative on the outskirts of the town with the haymaking.

In 1860 Hayle was one step ahead of St. Ives as it had a Battery of Artillery Volunteers, while St. Ives did not, and in July the Mayor of St. Ives, Mr. R. Kernick, was asked to arrange a public meeting to take steps towards the formation of a St. Ives Corps. It is not known if this was due to civic pride or the fact that a new three-gun battery was soon to be installed on the Island, and despite objections by some Church leaders that it would desecrate the Sabbath and result in a variety of unspecified evils, the proposal was received with acclamation. Early in September the newly formed unit had a chance of seeing the new guns in action for the first time. The large gun was fired first, the 68 pound ball passing close over the target — a rock some 1500 yards away. Shells were then fired from the two smaller guns, both of which fell short. The last shot rebounded from the sea, struck a rock and landed on the Island where it exploded near some cows — a display which appears to have anticipated Barnes Wallis's 'bouncing bombs'.

The swearing-in of the volunteers by the Deputy Lieutenant of the County, Mr. T.S. Bolitho, was a grand occasion. It was a fine afternoon, most of the shops were closed and the town had a holiday atmosphere. The members and friends met at the Town Hall, from where they proceeded to the Parish Church for a service, then back to the Town Hall for the swearing-in. To show his practical support Mr. Bolitho presented the Corps with a suitably inscribed silver bugle. They all then marched down to the Island where they were met by members of the Hayle Volunteers who had given great encouragement and support to the St. Ives men in the formation of their Corps. The Hayle Corps demonstrated some drill exercises, then to the strains of their fife and drum band led a procession to the Western Hotel where they and their friends had dinner. The St. Ives contingent moved on to the National Schools where they and their friends had dinner, and in the evening the St. Ives Choral Society gave a concert for funds towards the St. Ives fife and drum band, a concert which was well attended and gave great satisfaction. By this time Bombardier Macdonald had arrived for the purpose of drilling members of the Corps, and Messrs. Bolitho generously placed a portion of their large seine lofts at the disposal of the Corps for indoor drill.

The Island Garrison with the gun battery behind. One of the three firing positions now holds the National Coastwatch Institute's St. Ives watchkeeping station. The watch station is just visible above the grass bank on the left, beside the flag pole.

It was not until October that they got around to formally electing the Officers, followed by establishing the unit on 8th November. Mr. Robert Snaith Hichens became Captain, Mr. John Newman Tremearne, 1st Lieutenant, Mr. Charles Granville Grenfell, 2nd Lieutenant and Mr. D. F. Stevens, Surgeon. Also appointed were Sergeants, Corporals and Bombardiers, and the Rev. R. F. Tyacke as Chaplain.

When researching the *St. Ives Weekly Summary* for an article on the visit of the Duke of Cornwall's Light Infantry Regiment to St. Ives in 1899 I came across the following list of the officers who had served in the St. Ives Battery of the Duke of Cornwall's Artillery Volunteers between being set up in 1860 to being disbanded in 1878. The list also indicated that during that period 255 members were enrolled in it.

> *Robert Snaith Hichens*, Captain on formation 8th November 1860; resigned 27th June 1861; re-appointed as 2nd Lieutenant 23rd June 1863; resigned 7th February 1865.
>
> *John Newman Tremearne*, 1st Lieutenant on formation, 8th November 1860; resigned 30th November 1861; re-appointed as Captain 5th April 1870 vice Grenfell resigned; resigned 30th December 1871.
>
> *Charles Granville Grenfell*, 2nd Lieutenant on formation 8th November 1860; Captain 26th June 1861 vice Hichens resigned; resigned 6th April 1870.
>
> *William Hichens*, 2nd Lieutenant 26th June 1861 vice Grenfell promoted; 1st Lieutenant 30th November 1861 vice Tremearne resigned; resigned 23rd June 1863.
>
> *William Cade*, 2nd Lieutenant 26th June 1861 vice Hichens promoted; 1st Lieutenant 23rd June 1863 vice Hichens resigned; resigned 11th December 1869.
>
> *Richard Francis Treweeke*, 2nd Lieutenant 18th March 1865 vice Cade resigned; resigned 6th April 1870.
>
> *Richard Cogar*, 1st Lieutenant 5th April 1870; resigned 30th December 1871.
>
> *Charles Curnow*, 2nd Lieutenant 5th April 1870 vice Treweeke resigned; resigned May 1878.
>
> *Edward G. Davenport*, Captain 2nd August 1873 vice Tremearne resigned; died 4th December 1874.

Ed. Fitzgerald, Sub-Lieutenant 2nd August 1873; Captain March 1875 vice Davenport deceased; resigned 23rd June 1876.

To my mind, the star of the Volunteers was the Drum Major and Band Master of the Corps, Thomas Mathews, described in the following words by his great-nephew, John Hobson Matthews:

My great-uncle, Thomas Matthews, born 1791, having been apprenticed to his father in the business of a shipbuilder, was employed in the Government Dock-yards of Woolwich and Portsmouth. He afterwards became a Warrant-Officer and Gunnery Instructor in the Coastguard. He had been a member of the First Volunteer Force of 1812, and, when the New Volunteer movement arose the Saint Ives officers were anxious to include the old man in their battery of the Cornish Artillery. As he was a skilful musician, they made him Bandmaster and Drum Major, and he taught nearly every instrument that was used in the band, as also the fife (he played the bass-viol at church, too).

When the regiment paraded, it was a grand sight to see the veteran, in all the gilded glory of the Drum Major's uniform, waving his baton majestically at the head of the column. Every boy in West Cornwall envied Mr. Mathews on these occasions. He was of a very choleric temperament. Dr D F Stevens (Surgeon to the Corps) told me that one day, when the Volunteers were marching down The Terrace, headed by the band, the Drum Major was greatly impeded by a lot of girls, who persisted in walking just in front of him. Losing his patience at last, he pushed the baton between the legs of the biggest girl, from behind, and lifted her bodily onto the side of the road. Someone remarking to him that he had been rather rough, he sharply replied: 'If it had been my own father I would have done the same.'

His bodily strength was very great. A waggon once stuck in a rut at the bottom of the High Street, Saint Ives. Several men ineffectually tried to draw out the wheel. Uncle Thomas came along, and saying 'Stand aside,' put his shoulder to the wheel and lifted it out of the rut in a trice.

He was a big, broad-chested man, with white hair and beard, and had a voice of tremendous power. He was a noted base (sic) singer, and was in consider-able request at public concerts etc. On one occasion he took part in a musical festival at Winchester Cathedral, where his children went to hear him sing. He had to sing in the base duet The Lord is a Man of War *and when his tremendous voice rang through the building, one of his daughters exclaimed, in a startled tone: 'What is Father scolding us for now?' Great-uncle Thomas Mathews, in his closing years, was present at a Volunteer dinner given at Saint Ives, and, as the senior member of the corps, got up to propose the health of the Duke of Cornwall's Volunteer Artillery. Getting somewhat confused in his ideas, as the speech proceeded, he suddenly began to inveigh against the bogey of his youth, Napoleon Buonaparte, whom he denounced and defied in tones of thunder. 'Let him come,' cried the veteran, 'let him come if he dare, and I will be in the front rank to oppose him!'*

The old Drum Major died at Falmouth in 1863, of a violent cold caught in consequence of his going out, on a very wet day, in spite of the warnings and remonstrances of his family, to superintend the firing of a salute in honour of the Prince of Wales' wedding.

★★★★★

What a man!

Permission to quote John Hobson Matthews' description of the Drum Major was by courtesy of his grand-daughter, Miss Vivien Matthews. It is contained in what is known by the Matthews' family as 'the Fat Book,' a very large volume of miscellaneous information including records of many St. Ives families as well as local historical matters. The contents are now on fiche, generously donated by Miss Matthews to the St. Ives Archive Study Centre.

ROBERT LOUIS STEVENSON
& the CORNISH CONNECTION

Robert Louis Stevenson (R.L.S.) is known to many people only through a handful of his writings, for example *Treasure Island, Kidnapped* or *Dr. Jekyll and Mr. Hyde*, but his output was prodigious. Over a period of about 40 years he produced some 400 pieces of prose and enough personal letters to fill eight large volumes published by Yale University. His life and works have been the subject of research and analysis by many eminent writers and historians and one could be forgiven for thinking that everything that could be said about him has been said.

I have, however, been interested in an aspect which does not appear to have been investigated by the experts — a connection with Cornwall and the Cornish which might account for the following comment which appeared in an essay *Across the Plains* in which he described his journey on an emigrant train from New York to San Francisco:-

> *'There were no emigrants direct from Europe — save one German family and a knot of Cornish miners who kept grimly to themselves, one reading the New Testament all day long through steel spectacles, the rest discussing privately the secrets of their old-world, mysterious race. Lady Hester Stanhope believed she could make something great of the Cornish; for my part, I can make nothing of them at all. A division of races, older and more original than that of Babel, keeps this close, esoteric family apart from neighbouring Englishmen. Not even a Red Indian seems more foreign in my eyes. This is one of the lessons of travel — that some of the strangest races dwell next door to you at home . . .'*

Reading this as a Cornishman I was interested to try to find out what it was about us that so discomfited R.L.S.; what connections he may have had with Cornwall which could have influenced his attitude, so much in contrast to that of Lady Stanhope.

Wherever he went R.L.S. was interested in the nature of the people with whom he came into contact. While paddling his canoe on waterways in northern France and travelling in the mountains and forests of the Cevennes with Modestine, his

111

donkey, he had definite views on the French. The inhabitants of New York provoked mixed reactions. In California he commented on the Mexicans in the old California capital of Monterey, the Chinese in San Francisco, the Germans and Jews in the former mining town of Silverado where he spent his honeymoon in the ruins of a silver mine where Cornish miners had worked, and when he finally settled in Samoa he established such a rapport with the natives that they called him Tusitala, the teller of tales.

In 1879, although a sick man, and against the advice of friends, he set out from Scotland to go to America to join the lady whom he would marry. The voyage from Glasgow to New York was wonderfully described in *From the Clyde to Sandy Hook* and reading his account of the conditions endured by steerage passengers one cannot help wondering how Richard Jose of Lanner managed. At the age of fourteen he was put on a train at Redruth by his widowed mother, with an address label attached to his jacket, to make his way to his uncle in a mining camp in Virginia City, Nevada. Richard sang his way to Virginia City, only to find his relative had died, but he survived and became one of the finest tenors in the U.S.A.

Stevenson sailed from Glasgow on the *Devonia*, one of the Anchor line fleet, which carried 51 first class, 22 second class and 183 steerage passengers. He travelled 2nd Cabin, which gave him a table on which to write — a daily occupation which caused much amusement to the steerage passengers. He had no communication with the first class passengers but mixed freely with those in the steerage, joining in the communal activities, mainly singing, and all the time observing what was going on.

There were no Cornish miners on the *Devonia*. The ship's manifest, the original of which is in the New York Public Library, includes miners from Scotland, but none from England. On the steamship *Bristol,* which arrived in New York from Bristol shortly before the *Devonia* however, there was a group of four English miners and their families, named Wren (or perhaps Uren), Champion, Hardy and Pearson. These may have been the 'knot of Cornish miners' but unless anyone has a record of their mining ancestors having travelled on that particular emigrant train with R.L.S., we shall never know.

The description of the train journey R.L.S. made across America in his essay *Across the Plains* illustrates the discomforts, and in many cases the disillusionment, suffered by the emigrants hoping for a better life in the New World. Not everyone, however, was heading for the Golden West. R.L.S. comments that as he and his companions continued to steam westward they were continually passing other emigrant trains upon the journey east whose passengers urged them to '*Come back!*' The accounts of the voyage and the train journey were subsequently published in one book *The Amateur Emigrant*.

As far I can ascertain R.L.S. had very little connection with Cornwall. The first reference is in a letter from his home at 17 Heriot Row, Edinburgh to his friend Sidney Colvin on 2nd August 1877 in which he said '. . . *I shan't be able to come to Yorkshire for I'm to be whipped away tomorrow to Penzance . . .*'. His mother's diary recorded that R.L.S. and his parents left Edinburgh on 3rd August and travelled to Cornwall by way of Carlisle, Hereford, Gloucester and Exeter. At each place they visited and admired the cathedral. They arrived at Penzance in the evening of 7th August and put up at The Queen's Hotel on the Promenade.

Having admired all the cathedrals on the way south Mrs. Stevenson was not so complimentary about Cornwall, of which she said in her diary '. . . *Don't admire Cornwall at all . . .*' They were, however, very comfortable at The Queen's Hotel, with a fine sea view and bracing and delicious air. The following day they visited St. Michael's Mount with friends, then to the Logan Rock and Land's End — a fine day, which they enjoyed very much. The next day they sailed again to the Mount and Mrs. Stevenson commented '*We like Penzance better than we expected when we arrived . . .*'

The visits to the Mount may have been influenced by an essay R.L.S. had in mind or perhaps the idea for the essay came from the visits. Back in the Hotel R.L.S. wrote to his friend Frances Sitwell, referring to the considerable amount of literary work he had in hand '. . . *also in the clouds, or perhaps a little further away, an essay on the 'Two St. Michael's Mounts', historical and picturesque: perhaps if it didn't come too long I might throw in the Bass Rock, and call it 'Three Sea Fortalices' or something of that kind . . .*'

In the same letter to Sitwell R.L.S. said '. . . *Cornwall is not much to my taste, being as bleak as the bleakest parts of Scotland and nothing like so pointed and characteristic. It has a flavour of its own, though, which I may try to catch, if I can find the space, in the proposed article . . .*', and he ends with '. . . *Love to all. I must stop — going to Land's End*'. Among his papers at Yale University are notes on St. Michael's Mount and Mont St. Michel which he made from Fortescue Hitchin's *The History of Cornwall* (1824) and F.G.B. Manet's *État Ancien et de l'état actuel de la baie du Mont Saint-Michel* (1828). It appears however that the essay was not written, which is a pity, as it would no doubt have thrown light on his attitude towards the Cornish.

On Sunday 12th August the family attended Church at Newlyn, a very high choral service, which Mrs. Stevenson did not like. On Monday they drove to Gurnard's Head — nice rocks but nothing wonderful. The following day R.L.S. and his mother sailed to the Scilly Isles and stayed at the Inn at Hugh Town, where they admired the flowers and shrubs in the garden. Because of wet weather the next day they did not make a planned visit to Tresco and as R.L.S. developed toothache they cut short their stay and returned to Penzance.

On the 16th August, nine days after arriving at Penzance, R.L.S. left to join his artist friends at Grez-sur-Loing in the forest of Fontainebleau on the outskirts of Paris, while Mr. and Mrs. Stevenson drove to Mousehole. There are no further references to Cornwall in Mrs. Stevenson's diaries and she and her husband continued their tour from Cornwall into Devon, arriving back in Edinburgh on 29th August. R.L.S. did not return from France until the 18th November.

R.L.S.'s father, Thomas, was one of the Stevenson family of lighthouse engineers and I had hoped that as a result of the links between the Commissioners of Northern Lights in Scotland and Trinity House in England he might have been invited to visit some of the Cornish lights, but there is no record of this.

So what of Lady Hester Stanhope who took a more optimistic attitude towards the Cornish? Lady Hester was what would be described as an English eccentric, who travelled widely in the Middle East and built herself a palace in the Lebanon Range. She was once visited by Alexander William Kinglake, a banker and solicitor of Taunton, Somerset. Kinglake was more interested in military history than banking. He had followed the English expedition to the Crimea during which he became acquainted with Lord Raglan and subsequently wrote an 8-volume history of the Crimean War. He had long philosophical discussions with Lady Hester and in an account of his meeting with her he said '. . . *One favourite subject of discourse was that of 'race'. Upon this she was very diffuse, and yet rather mysterious. She set great value on the ancient French, not Norman, blood (for that she vilified) but professed to despise the*

St. Michael's Mount, visited by Robert Louis Stevenson and his mother in 1877 when they stayed at the Queens Hotel, Penzance. St. Michael's Mount and its French counterpart Mont St Michel are the subject of notes in the RLS collection at Yale University.

English notion of 'an old family'. She had a vast idea of the Cornish miners on account of their race, and said, if she chose, she could give me the means of rousing them to the most tremendous enthusiasm . . .'

Sadly she apparently did not choose to disclose to Alexander her means of rousing the Cornish to the most tremendous enthusiasm, and unlike present-day interviewers he did not press her.

My problem with Stevenson, a Scotsman, is reconciling his views on the Cornish in 1879 with the only reference I can find to Cornwall — his visit to the County two years previously. A nine-day visit to West Cornwall which included a bout of toothache and wet weather hardly seems enough to produce a balanced judgment on the temperament of the Cornish as a race, but R.L.S. was quick to make judgments and if this visit was the only occasion on which he had any experience of the Cornish it can only be assumed that he struck a bad patch with the folk he met. How, for instance, could he know, from the vast numbers of emigrants, that the men on the emigrant train were miners and that they were Cornish? How also, was he aware of Lady Stanhope's views? From the Pacific Transfer Station near Council Bluffs, on the eastern bank of the Missouri river, the emigrants moved to the Emigrant House, where an official read their names from a list before they boarded the train. It seems unlikely the official would call for 'Tom Richards, tin miner, St. Ives, Cornwall,' and if the group of men kept themselves to themselves it is difficult to see how Stevenson could have reached his conclusion. Perhaps the answer lies buried somewhere in the eight volumes of letters residing in the Library of Yale University.

73 YEARS ON
SS Trevessa *remembered*

The SS Trevessa

Photograph: St. Ives Museum Collection

The recent International Festival of the Sea at Bristol was a great success and Bristol Docks were crowded with some 700 craft of all sizes, from coracles and Cornish racing gigs to magnificent tall ships, although it wasn't possible to do what could be done years ago in St. Ives harbour — walk from one side to the other across their decks. Working boats, sail training vessels, Navy ships and pleasure craft were all there. It was a truly international affair with boats from countries as far afield as U.S.A. and Russia, and the former St. Ives lugger *Our John* was among them. The sight of the Cathedral and the Cabot Tower through a forest of masts and riggings gave an idea of what it must have looked like a hundred years ago when Bristol was a major maritime city and tall ships came right up into the City centre.

Excellent pasties were available in the Cornwall refreshment tent and it was good to see four enterprising St. Ives businesses attracting much public attention in the Cornwall pavilion. Leon Pezzack of Mousehole, working on the blade of a racing oar alongside one of his beautiful gigs, was also the centre of interest, while the Falmouth Marine Band with their marching, whistles, cymbals, drums and no music entertained and bemused the crowds.

There was extensive television coverage of the boats and the dozens of fringe activities in the Festival, which included a public auction of nautical items by a leading London auction house. One item in the auction which caused much interest for the cameras, was a collection of documents and photographs related to events following the loss of the Hain steamship *Trevessa* in the Indian Ocean in 1923. The collection had been put together by an unidentified survivor and included his account of his experiences in one of the lifeboats. With a guide price of £60 to £80 the bidding opened at £1,000 with a number of telephone bidders competing with those in the marquee. Offers rose rapidly and closed at £2,300 to a telephone bidder.

For anyone with any knowledge of Sir Edward Hain and the Hain Steamship Company of St. Ives the very name *Trevessa* recalls a dramatic story of disaster, courage, discipline and great seamanship. The lessons learned by the crew in navigation schools and the practical experience gained in Hain steamships around the world were sorely tested and the results were in the very best traditions of seafarers and the Merchant Service. The story also recalls the kindness and support shown to the survivors by the inhabitants of the islands of Rodriguez and Mauritius.

The vessel was built in Germany in 1909 for a German shipping line and was named *Imkenturm*. She was interned in the Dutch East Indies during the first world war and was taken over by the Shipping Controller in 1919. In 1920 she was sold to the Hain Steamship Company and renamed *Trevessa,* the second vessel in the Hain fleet to bear that name, with the large white H on her funnel, having been fully surveyed and reconditioned and her German steel lifeboats replaced by four newly built British wooden craft.

The final fatal voyage of the *Trevessa* under the command of Capt. Cecil Foster of Barry, South Wales, started on May 15th 1923 when she left Port Pirie, South Australia with a cargo of zinc concentrates bound for Antwerp via Fremantle and Durban. Some of the crew were apprehensive as to their chances of getting home, not because of any doubts regarding the vessel, but their sailormen's superstitions associated with cats. A black cat adopted in Port Pirie jumped ship before they sailed. Another cat had previously left the ship in New Zealand. Capt. Foster subsequently related how he had disposed of two kittens from a batch of six black ones, although he eased the crew's misgivings by assuring them they were not completely black as they had white patches on the chest. Between Port Pirie and Fremantle a favourite tabby cat died on board before giving birth to her kittens and finally, when the crew were in the lifeboats, the cat they took with them jumped back on to the sinking ship.

After they left Fremantle on May 25th the weather deteriorated but despite the worsening sea conditions the ship behaved well. On June 3rd, however, in a severe SSW gale a huge sea tore the two port lifeboats from their lashings and it was only with great difficulty that they were secured. At about midnight it was realised the ship was labouring and appeared to be down by the head, investigations indicating there was a leak in the forward hold and the bulkheads were bulging. By 12.45 am the water was at the top of the forward hold. At 1.00 am on June 4th Capt. Foster sent an SOS message with their position and that they would be abandoning ship. As many additional provisions as they could manage, mainly condensed milk, biscuits and extra water breakers, were put aboard the two starboard lifeboats, a procedure which in itself carried considerable risks. By 2.15am the ship was floating level with the bulwarks and was abandoned. Half an hour later she foundered.

Because of the possibility that the port lifeboats had been damaged the starboard lifeboats were used, which involved manoeuvring the ship to enable the boats to be lowered as safely as was possible. With the rudder out of the water and little help from the propeller this required great skill with seas running at 20 to 30 feet and winds from force 7 to 9. All 44 members of the ship's company were accommodated in the two lifeboats, twenty in No.1 boat under the command of Capt. Foster and twenty-four in No.3 boat under Chief Officer Smith. Two of *Trevessa*'s sister ships, *Tregenna* and *Trevean,* picked up the SOS and diverted to the scene, but despite extensive searches found no trace of survivors and it was thought there was little chance of finding any of the crew alive although Capt. Dunnett of the *Trevean* remained optimistic.

For several days the two lifeboats kept company, heading for Mauritius some 1700 miles to the north-west, taking advantage of wind and tide, but on June 9th as no rescue vessels were in sight it was agreed that as boat No.1 was faster they should separate and whichever reached land or was rescued first would seek help for the other. If they missed the islands of Rodriguez or Mauritius and were not rescued by a passing ship the next landfall would be Madagascar, but it was unlikely the rations would last that long. Capt. Foster said: '. . . *We parted with cheers and the chorus ringing from either boat: 'Are we down-hearted?' the answer 'No' being given heartily'*. In the event boat No.1 covered 1556 miles and boat No.3 1747 miles.

Capt. Foster in his book *1700 miles in open boats. The story of the loss of the S.S. Trevessa in the Indian Ocean, and the voyage of her boats to safety* has vividly told the story of the subsequent days, with extracts from daily logs kept by him and Chief Officer Smith, a story of endurance, improvisation and seamanship. At 2.45 pm on June 26th the Captain's boat sighted land which proved to be Rodriguez Island, part of the Mascerene islands, 334 miles east of Mauritius, literally a spot in the ocean being 13 miles long and three to six miles wide. There the crew were kindly treated and given medical attention, news of their safe arrival being transmitted by the Eastern Telegraph Company, and *H.M.S. Colombo* stationed at Mauritius was despatched to pick them up. On arrival at Rodriguez the Captain of the Colombo was briefed as to the likely course taken by boat No.3 and immediately set out to search for them, but returned when news was received that they had reached Mauritius.

After parting company with the Captain's boat on June 9th, Chief Officer Smith in boat No.3 kept going and as he was unable to reach the island of Rodriguez due to the weather conditions he made for Mauritius. On the afternoon of June 28th land was sighted and recognised to be the island of Mauritius by the mountain Pieter Both above the main town of Port Louis. On nearing the island their landing at Bel Ombre at the very southern tip was delayed for several hours due to difficulties in finding a passage through a coral reef but with help from local fishermen they made it the following morning. The survivors were carried ashore on stretchers and taken to a temporary hospital on the nearby sugar estate from where they were later transferred to the military hospital on the island. They were well looked after, and when the Colombo returned from Rodriguez there was a joyful re-union tempered by sadness at the loss of comrades on the two voyages.

Capt. Foster recorded that of the 44 members of the ship's company 11 men were lost following the abandonment of the ship, two from the Captain's boat due to exposure and exhaustion and nine from that of the Chief Officer. Of those nine, one fell overboard and could not be saved, seven died at sea from exposure and exhaustion, and the ship's cook died in hospital shortly after arrival at Mauritius, again as a result of exposure and exhaustion. Although exhorted that under no circumstances should they drink seawater some of those who died had succumbed to the temptation. During their stay on Mauritius the survivors were overwhelmed with acts of kindness and generosity. A memorial and thanksgiving service was held in St. James' Cathedral on July 11th and it was with mixed feelings that they left for home on the 16th.

On July 16th 1923 the survivors of the *Trevessa* set out for home on the *R.M.S.Ghoorkha* and were besieged by pressmen at Durban and Cape Town. As they approached Gravesend on August 23rd they found all the vessels there dressed with flags and blowing their sirens, and below Gravesend they were joined by many relatives. After official welcomes and lunch the men proceeded to the Tilbury Board of Trade office where they were discharged from their ship's articles and were at liberty to go home to their families. The Captain, Chief Officer and Chief Engineer met the Directors of the Hain Steamship Company at their office where Capt. Foster was presented with a silver tea tray, Chief Officer Smith with a silver rose bowl and Chief Engineer Robson with a silver inkstand, each with appropriate inscriptions.

On January 15th 1924 Capt. Foster and Chief Officer Smith were received at Buckingham Palace where the King and Queen congratulated them on their success in coming through and asked many questions about their experiences. Further presentations were made by the President of the Board of Trade - a silver tea service (to go with the tray) for Capt. Foster and a silver inkstand for Chief Officer Smith. Boat No.1 was bought by the Anglo-Ceylon Estates Company Limited of Mauritius and brought to England where it was set up in the grounds of the Ceylon Court of the British Empire Exhibition at Wembley. The telephone bidder at the auction in Bristol now has an interesting collection of memorabilia of the *Trevessa*, but where, I wonder, are the log books, the silver tea service, the silver tray, the rose bowl, the inkstands and boat No.1?

The story is one of endurance and although they suffered many privations Capt. Foster and Chief Officer Smith continually supported and encouraged their companions. In his book Capt. Foster said:

'. . . During these last days sometimes one, sometimes another, would get a bit pessimistic and say he could not last much longer. I used to tell them that I intended to get in and that it was up to them to stick it out, and that was sufficient. Every man had to do his bit and do it to the limit of his strength and capacity. Every man was 'all out,' both mentally and physically, and those who were better equipped than the others in either or both ways never hinted that they might be doing more than their share when they were called upon to exert their powers to the utmost . . .'

This attitude was acknowledged by the formal Inquiries on Mauritius and in London, both of which expressed admiration for the fine seamanship and resolution of the officers and the splendid discipline and courage of the crew.

No St. Ives men were among the crew on this particular voyage of the *Trevessa*, but on Rodriguez Capt. Foster met a Mr. Hearne from St. Ives, also Mr. E. Richards, eldest son of Capt. and Mrs. E. Richards of Rosevale, St. Ives, who was an employee of the Eastern Telegraph Company and who despatched the following cable to the folk at home: *'Capt. Foster and rest Trevessa's crew send best wishes St. Ives. Convey sympathy to Mrs. Sparks Lelant'*.

Harry Sparks was aged 19 and the son of Capt. and Mrs. Sparks of Lelant. He had associations with the West Cornwall Golf Club and was one of five apprentices on the ship. He died in boat No.3 four days before they reached Mauritius, and Chief Officer Smith said of him *'Up to about a week before his death, that is to say as long as his strength lasted, Sparks had taken his turn at the helm and had helped to steer the boat'*. The memorial service at Lelant Church was attended by Mr. Arthur Tippett of Penzance, 3rd Officer, himself a survivor, along with Mr. Guy Williams of Lelant, at that time serving on the *Trevorian* and Chief Officer of the *Trevessa* until her last voyage. Two other Hain apprentices, Messrs. J. Daniel and J. Vivian of Redruth, at that time on the *Treneglos,* also attended, as well HRH The Ranee of Sarawak who lived in the village and representatives of Lord Inchcape and the Hain Line Directors.

As well as Arthur Tippett, other crew members from West Cornwall who survived were R.J. McKenzie, messroom steward of St. Just, and Eric W.J. Goddard, apprentice, of the Isles of Scilly, who also took his turn at steering the boat. One man, well known in St. Ives at that time, perhaps owed his life to breaking his

The Captains Boat (No.1) was bought by the Anglo-Ceylon Estates Company of Mauritius, who brought it to England where it was set up in the grounds of the Ceylon Court of the British Empire Exhibition at Wembley 1924-25. Sadly, if it exists its present whereabouts are unknown. The collection box was presumably on behalf of Missions to Seamen.

1700 Miles in Open Boats, *Captain Cecil Foster 1924*

leg. Mr. J.W. Jones, third officer of the *Trevessa*, who lived at Lostwithiel, broke his leg while playing football at Lostwithiel early in December 1922 and as a result did not sail on what was to be her last voyage.

In a recent letter to *The Daily Telegraph* Mr. Ian Bell, writing from Singapore, suggests that his father, the late Sir Douglas Bell CBE who was an apprentice on the *Trevessa* (he too took his turn at the helm) and one of the survivors, was probably unaware that Mauritius still celebrates *Trevessa Day*. He is not the only one, but enquiries are under way to find out what happens and when.

As the Hain Steamship Company originated in St. Ives and was so closely involved with the town, with many St. Ives men employed by the Company as Captains and crew, I wonder if there would be merit in an annual *Hain Day* in St. Ives to co-incide with *Trevessa Day* in Mauritius. While there are still those in retirement who sailed on Hain steamships it would offer an opportunity for a re-union, and a short service in the harbour area would remember those who lost their lives at sea, whether far away in the Indian Ocean or nearer home, as well as offering thanks for the help extended to the survivors of the *Trevessa* by the islanders of Rodriguez and Mauritius. It would be an opportunity to remind our grandchildren and inform our visitors of an important part of the town's history with a lecture or two on the Hain family, the Steamship Company and the vessels.

Other events could be a regatta, a Lifeboat day, an open-day on a minesweeper, exhibitions of maritime paintings by well-remembered artists of the St. Ives school, showings of slides and appropriate films, including the Barnes brothers' classics and a performance of *The Pirates of Penzance* or *HMS Pinafore*. Mix these ingredients and *Hain Day* could become part of a St. Ives Festival of the Sea. That would indeed be a day or days for flying the flags from the Lodges!

Survivors of SS Trevessa *with Mr. Brodie, agent for the Hain Steamship Company and Rev. Golding-Bird, Bishop of Mauritius, after a combined thanksgiving and memorial service held in St. James' Cathedral on 11th July 1923.*
1700 Miles in Open Boats, *Captain Cecil Foster 1924*

UPDATE on SS *TREVESSA*
& Seafarers Day on Mauritius

*T*he *St. Ives Times & Echo* of 4th October 1996 carried a report of a meeting between Capt. John Kemp MBE and Lady Phyllis Bell, widow of the late Sir Douglas Bell CBE, who, with Capt. Kemp, was an apprentice on the *SS Trevessa*. Another successful meeting has recently taken place, this time between Capt. Kemp and Ian Bell, the son of Sir Douglas and Lady Bell, who travelled specially from Singapore to St. Ives to meet and talk with his father's friend and shipmate. These meetings were some of the outcomes of my articles on the *Trevessa* in the *St. Ives Times & Echo* on 5th and 12th July last year, in which reference was made to enquiries regarding the annual *Trevessa Day* on the island of Mauritius, enquiries which have produced interesting information, including photographs and other material.

Capt. Kemp is central to the story of the *Trevessa* as he may well be the only man alive who sailed on her from the day she was commissioned as a Hain steamer, although he did not sail on that final fatal voyage, and I have had the privilege of talking with him about his experiences. St. Ives born and bred he entered the service of the Hain Steamship Company at the age of 15¼, and travelled to South Shields on January 9th 1921 to join the *Trevessa* as one of five apprentices, all aged between 15 and 17. He recalls how his mother went to St. Erth with him where he joined Eric Goddard from the Scilly Isles, another *Trevessa* apprentice, on the train to Newcastle. His mother would then follow his whereabouts through the weekly lists of Hain steamer movements in *The St. Ives Times*.

A week later *Trevessa* left the Tyne under the command of Capt. W.H. Gibson and did not return until the beginning of September, during which time they called at ports in Europe, India and the Far East. Less than a fortnight later they were off again on their way to Colombo, and on Capt. Kemp's 16th birthday *Trevessa* was on passage from Calcutta to Rangoon. On Christmas Day they were at Delagoa Bay, Portuguese East Africa, a far cry from the churches and chapels of St. Ives and the rounds of the Cock Robin choirs.

Many St. Ives families will recall in their homes paintings of Italian scenes including Vesuvius in eruption, brought back from Italy by crew members. When foreign ships docked at Italian ports it was common for local artists to approach the crew with offers to paint their particular ship onto pre-painted scenes. Each apprentice on the *Trevessa* bought a painting of the ship in Genoa for ten shillings. Capt Kemp's still has pride of place in his home.

The *Trevessa* was an ex-German ship and the apprentices had the luxury of two-berth cabins on the after-deck rather than a communal dormitory, but apprenticeship on a Hain steamer was no soft option. They signed on for periods of two, three or four years, and during that time they agreed, among other things, to keep their Master's secrets, not to embezzle or waste his goods, not to frequent Taverns or Alehouses except on his business, and not to play unlawful games. They had technical instruction, with written work, under the guidance of the Captain and the First Officer and were involved in all aspects of the working of the ship other than navigation. When a senior apprentice died of malaria, John Kemp assisted the First Officer, Mr. Guy Williams of Lelant, to sew up the body in a canvas sheet with lead weights prior to burial at sea. A chilling experience for a 16-year old but an experience the other apprentices would encounter later in the lifeboats, except that then there would be no canvas sheets and no lead weights.

One of the first tasks given the apprentices after they left the Tyne was cleaning the brass on the poop, the worst position on the ship in stormy weather. As the ship had been laid up for four years in a tropical climate large amounts of elbow grease and cleaning paste were involved. They prepared the paste in the lamp room by crushing bath brick and mixing it with colza oil which was used for the ship's lanterns. 'Brasso' was expensive and reserved for the final polish.

Apprentice John Kemp served on the *Trevessa* until the 28th December 1922 when she dry-docked at Liverpool and he then transferred to the *Tregothnan*, another of the Hain fleet. At the same time Capt. C. Foster took over command from Capt. Gibson and only four of the original crew who set out from the Tyne two years previously rejoined the ship — the 2nd and 3rd Engineers and two apprentices, Douglas Bell and Eric Goddard.

Capt. Kemp obtained his Master's ticket at the age of 25 and in 1930 left the Hain Company to join the Glasgow-based Andrew Weir "Bank" Line where he commanded vessels which took him all over the world until he retired in 1970. During the Second World War he served in the Royal Navy and in 1960 was awarded the M.B.E. for humanitarian efforts in evacuating refugees from Colombo in connection with the 1958 rioting.

In May 1963, while on a voyage from Japan to Cape Town with a new vessel *M.V. Inverbank*, on which he was accompanied by his wife Ann, the ship called at Mauritius to discharge cargo. While there they drove to Bel Ombre, the point at the southern end of the island where *Trevessa*'s boat No.3 made landfall, to pay their respects at the memorial which had been erected by the islanders. They were especially welcome, coming from St. Ives and with Capt. Kemp's connection with the *Trevessa*, and were invited to stay for *Trevessa Day*, but had to continue the voyage to Cape Town.

On the *Trevessa* John Kemp shared an apprentice cabin with Douglas Bell from Glasgow, and they became friends. The connection with Douglas Bell moved the enquiry to Singapore, to his son Mr. Ian Bell, whose letter to *The Daily Telegraph* at the time of the Bristol auction prompted my enquiry regarding *Trevessa Day*. Douglas Bell obtained his Master's ticket and continued to work for the Hain Company for several years until he transferred to the Gow Harrison Line of Glasgow where he was in command of tankers. During the great depression in the 1930's he and his ship were laid up for a long period in Rotterdam, where he met his future wife, and he left the sea to take up a new career in the steel industry, joining a major steel company in Scotland. He obtained his knighthood as a result of leading and managing a major consortium steelworks project at Durgapur in India, and died in 1974, not knowing that his friend and former shipmate Capt. Kemp was in St. Ives.

At the official Inquiry into the sinking of *Trevessa* apprentice Bell was given special praise. What was so special about him was partly his action in helping a fellow apprentice, Charles Seaborn, who was in his bunk, seriously ill with malaria. As the ship was sinking Captain Foster detailed Douglas Bell to ensure that Seaborn was brought safely to lifeboat No.3. He managed it and got him down the ropes into the boat. Charles Seaborn recovered after hospital treatment on Mauritius and never forgot that act by Douglas Bell, whose memory is still held in high regard by Seaborn's family.

Charles Seaborn joined the Hain Company on 23rd January 1920, when he was 17 and his Indenture which was for four years, was signed by Mr. McWilliams, the Hain Superintendent, and William Cogar, the Company Secretary in St. Ives. He served for short periods on the *Trevanion* and the *Tredinnick* before joining the *Trevessa* with the other apprentices. After recovering from his ordeal he went back to sea in the *Tregantle* and continued to serve in Hain steamers for the rest of his life at sea.

The only survivor to return to Mauritius, his first visit was in 1983 for *Trevessa Day*, the 60th anniversary of the landing and the day before his 80th birthday. His last visit was in 1991. Although blind in one eye and very frail he was determined to go back once more and was welcomed as the guest of honour by the island authorities. His daughter has kindly sent me a video of the 1991 *Trevessa Day* commemoration proceedings including her father being helped to lay a wreath at the memorial, followed by relaxation and hospitality at the Merchant Navy Club, an interesting and very moving piece of history. He died the following year. His last wish was that his ashes should be taken to Mauritius and scattered on the waters round the cape at Bel Ombre and his friends in Mauritius co-operated with his family in doing this.

Charles Seaborn kept in touch with Donald Lamont, the wireless operator, who went to live in New Zealand, and visited him there when on a cruise following his retirement. In the past few days I have been contacted by a relative of Donald Lamont who is also a relative of Ralph Flynn another apprentice survivor, and this will open up further enquiries. A letter from Ralph Flynn's mother and family in Plymouth was published in the *St. Ives Times* in July 1923, thanking all those who had rallied round during the anxious period following the news of the sinking and particularly Lord Inchcape, the Directors of the P&O and the Hain Line, and Messrs Read and Cogar at St. Ives, for their consideration and support.

So what of *Trevessa Day* itself? Captain Yves Goilot, Secretary of the Merchant Navy Club in Port Louis, has been most helpful in providing information. Those survivors who did not require hospital treatment were looked after by the Mauritius Sailors' Home Society (founded 1857) in the Sailors' Home in Port Louis. In 1957 the Home was modernised as the present Merchant Navy Club. At the same time it was decided that the annual *Trevessa Day* should be extended to remember seafarers generally — to quote the 1984 programme '. . . *a day set aside so that we may ponder on the fact that this Island is so deeply indebted to seafarers of many nations . . ,*' and the 29th June would in future be known as *Seafarers Day*. In 1957 ships were in port for about ten days, and seafarers had time to visit the Club. The day started with a Church Service, followed by the laying of wreaths at the Bel Ombre memorial and the grave of William Allchin, the ship's cook who died in hospital after landing. In the evening a party would be held, hosted by the Ships' Agents, to which all seafarers in port were invited.

In the early 1980's Port Louis shifted from being a lighterage port to a quay port with container ships starting to call there. With their reduced turnaround times the opportunities for crews to attend an evening function became restricted so it was abandoned. The ceremonies involving the Church and the laying of wreaths, however, continue annually. Further information will be forthcoming and Capt. Goilot makes the comment ' . . . *the suggestion of a link between St. Ives and Port Louis interests us - let's keep it afloat . . !*'

Text by Ted Fenna

The Trevessa *Trophy at the Royal Hong Kong Yacht Club*

You have walked past this magnificent trophy many times: it was in one of the trophy cabinets inside the main entrance. The *Trevessa* Trophy is a silver lifeboat, with sail, made by Po Cheung and carries plaques recording the winning ships and helms from 1924 to 1962, the last recorded race. Donated by Mr E Cock MBE, a Cornishman, and Commodore of the RHKYC in 1924, it was awarded to the winners of a rowing race in ships' lifeboats round Hong Kong harbour. The race apparently used to take about 3½ hours. Several of the names on the winners' plaques also appear in the list of *Trevessa* survivors.

The Trophy's history has recently come to light a as a result of research by Ian Bell, son of Douglas Bell, an apprentice on the *Trevessa,* and Cornishman historian Tom Richards. Two articles written by Richards appeared in *The St. Ives Times &*

Echo, and these prompted an historian at the University of Liverpool to send him an article written by a ship's officer on the S S *Anchises*, which described winning the *Trevessa Cup* on Boxing Day 1947 in Hong Kong harbour. RHKYC member Ted Fenna, through his Cornish connection, has also become involved in the story, and met up with Ian when the latter visited the Club with his wife in July this year.

There is substantial interest in resurrecting the race, and preliminary talks with the Ship Owners' Association of Hong Kong and the HK Sea School have been favourable, on condition that the race is a bit shorter. The story of the *Trevessa* is one of endurance, courage and fine seamanship, timeless qualities to be encouraged in every day and age.

After due consideration of present circumstances, not least the reduced size of Hong Kong harbour, it seems unlikely that the race will be revived.

Ian Bell and Capt. John Kemp MBE at Capt. Kemp's home in St. Ives, February 1997. Trevessa *painting in the background.*

THERE'S GOLD IN THEM THAR' PASTIES!
The Golden Pasty Award in Calumet, Michigan

One of the distractions of searching on the Internet is coming across something which you were not looking for but is worth investigating. Recently when looking for information on the Copper Range Railroad in the U.S.A. I found reference to it on a website devoted to the pasty, the last thing I would have associated with a railroad, so I diverted off the main line to see where it led. The result is a fascinating story of enterprise based on the town of Calumet in northern Michigan.

Copper had been mined in the Calumet area of the Keweena Peninsular, Michigan for centuries and Calumet was one of the first places in the United States of America where emigrants from Cornwall settled and found work in the mines. From 25,000 pounds of copper produced in 1845, production reached nearly 230 million in the peak year 1909. Before WW1 the whole of the production was bought by Germany, but in subsequent years demand fell, families moved on, particularly south to the auto factories of Detroit, and the Depression of 1932 put paid to the industry. The last mine closed in 1968 and in 1969 A .L. Rowse, in his book *The Cornish in America* said:

> *Today except for the most famous mine of all, the Calumet and Hecla combine, the place is even more derelict than the area around Camborne and Redruth; a shadow of what it once was, the forest closing in, mining villages empty, the miners' houses falling down, a few old people creeping about them; the haunts of the former folk given over to ghosts and memories . . .*

At the peak some 70,000 people lived in Calumet. Today the population is just over 800, made up of some 540 families. As with St. Ives, tourism is now the staple industry in Calumet, situated as it is in marvellous country near the shores of Lake Superior, but with it is the growth of a new industry based on the humble Cornish pasty.

Family recipes have been handed down from Cornish emigrants through the generations and for many years residents in the Still Waters Assisted Living Community in Calumet have made pasties as a regular activity, no doubt based on recipes from Cornish great-great-grandmothers, for their own consumption and selling locally as a fund-raiser. In 1995 Still Waters residents started selling their pasties on the Internet and as demand increased PastyNET Inc was incorporated in 1999. About 65 residents at the Home and 48 employees are now involved in the combined operation of producing and marketing the pasties.

At the turn of the century orders had reached about 20,000 pasties a year. By the summer of this year the number shipped exceeded 100,000, much of the demand from repeat orders, with shipments made by a dedicated carrier to cities and rural areas in 50 States. The pasties are shipped, deep-frozen, with special packaging which includes the *Mining Gazette* newspaper, a practical use for the preceding week's issue and advertising for the paper!

The net proceeds, after expenses, are used to fund a building upkeep reserve account, and along with tax-deductible gifts enable some much-needed repairs and replacements to be made at the Still Waters Home, while the residents benefit by the realisation that they participate in something of significance for others throughout North America.

So what is the connection between the Copper Range Railroad and a business making and selling pasties? The secret lies in the Golden Pasty Award, the brain-child of Charlie Hopper, Administrator of the Still Waters Community. The Great Lakes area generally relies on tourism, and the Pasty Central website, with its wide contacts seemed a good way of bringing to notice websites covering tourist attractions and local businesses noted for their technical excellence and their contribution to the area's economy. Anyone can nominate a website. Staff at Still Waters make their assessment and, if approved, give the website the Golden Pasty Award and a place on their Hall of Fame. The Copper Range Railroad is one of the most recent additions and is delighted at the honour and the publicity it brings. Non-profit community groups also feature, including class reunions, Cub Scouts and Church groups. One associated business, Grandmas Pasties in Bloomington, Minnesota, offers a pasty the like of which we have not yet seen even in the wide range on offer in St. Ives — the Breakfast Pasty, the ingredients being scrambled eggs, ham, potatoes and cheese.

Pasties are not the only Cornish fare produced in Calumet and widely distributed. The Thurner Bakery offers saffron rolls, much the same as our saffron buns, but I couldn't find reference to saffron cake — a gap in the market? It's a far cry from the days when Calumet exported copper to Germany to the present day with pasties distributed to 50 States in the U.S.A., but shows what enterprise can achieve in fund-raising for a worthy cause.

GHOSTS of CHRISTMAS PAST in ST IVES

Christmas is still hull-down over the horizon, but as the early voyagers to the New World knew they were approaching land by the sargasso weed in the sea, we know we are approaching Christmas by the advertisements for office party lunches and Four Days of Olde Worlde Festive Frolics. We will hear again that Christmas is not what it used to be. It will be too commercialised; the carols won't be as good; people will stay at home watching the telly and those who are out and about will be rowdy.

No doubt some of this will be true, but was it really so idyllic in the past, or was it only as good as we like to think it was? Like school holidays in the summer. Do you remember them, as I do, as six weeks of continuous sunshine, when we wore no shoes, went indoors only to eat and sleep, and you could tack a tin boat all day on Porthmeor beach without colliding with a single wind-break?

Let's have a look at what was happening in St. Ives for the Christmas period 1890 as recorded in the pages of the *St. Ives Weekly Summary and Visitors List*.

The first mention of Christmas was in the issue for Saturday, November 22nd, when Mr. James Uren White, who owned the *Summary*, advertised diaries, almanacks and annuals as well as 'Christmas Cards for Foreign Mails'. This was followed on December 13th by Mr. Lanham who offered 'useful goods suitable for the season' available in the general warehouse in High Street. Armed with Lanham's list there was no need for you to go to Penzance, Truro or Plymouth for most of your Christmas presents. You could buy a hammock-chair for mother; a silver-mounted French briar or a Meerschaum pipe for father. One granny could have a set of chamber ware, the other a bonnet box, with grandfathers having a chair-bed and a claret jug. Aunt Janie could have Berlin wool or fancy needlework in great variety, and Uncle Jimmy could entertain everyone with a new banjo.

While we may say that Christmas is a time for children, apart from Mr. White's advertisement for annuals there were none for children's toys — no Lego, no dolls who wet themselves and cry 'Mama' (never 'Dada') — but you could get Christmas tree ornaments in great variety, bon-bons and masks. If you were of a practical turn of mind and preferred to spend your money on the house, with next year's visitors in mind, Mr. Lanham could supply you with a brass bedstead, a Brussels tapestry or Kidder carpet, or a straw paliasse. He also had a picture gallery on the premises (admission free on presentation of a visiting card), but there was one notable omission from the list, which in years to come would be synonymous with the name of Lanham's of St. Ives — there was no mention of artists' materials. Liquid refreshment was in plentiful supply, ranging from claret at 1s.1d. a bottle, to quart flagons of Australian burgundy at 2s.6d., and 6-year old Glenlivet at 3s.7d a bottle. But don't get too excited about the prices — there was a vacancy for a Council Road Foreman at 18s.6d a week, and another for a general domestic servant at £8 a year, not much room for Glenlivet there! No shop in town these days can boast such an array of goodies, where you could come out with a bottle of port, meat and malt wine, a concertina and a set of strings for your violin, carried in a galvanised bath or washtub. Perhaps it's a question of demand as in a remote village shop in the Western Isles where the lady told me that visitors kept asking for a particular item and she kept telling them she didn't stock it because there was no demand!

What else was on offer? Mr. Guppy in Fore Street offered a boot and shoe department 'for the million,' with five percent discount for cash, while Mr. Comley along the road claimed to have the largest sale of boots and shoes in the neighbourhood. Mr. Simpson offered ready-made clothes and hats, and Mr. J.U. White seemed to offer just about everything from newspapers and magazines to window decoration with the appearance of real stained glass, memorial cards, a circulating library, insurance, Frith photographs, auction bills, dyeing with Pullars of Perth, and Mather's Nigrine, a jet black fluid for marking linen and cotton. Mr. Harris, general grocer opposite the Post Office in Fore Street, had Melton Mowbray sausages at 9d. a pound. You could also hire from him a landau, wagonette or dog cart.

The issue of January 3rd 1891 carried a brief report of the services and festivities, and mentioned the carol services at the Mariners', Wesleyan, Lady Huntingdon's and New Connection chapels. It said that the efforts of the various choirs were much appreciated and went on to say that the open-air carol singing, with one or two exceptions, was of a very low order. Oh dear! It also reported that ' . . . *there was the usual rowdy element in the streets — indeed we believe this year it was even worse than last. Sacred hymns were shouted in a most profane and irreverent manner and the conduct was extremely boisterous and unseemly. The behaviour was certainly not at all becoming for a Municipal Borough . . .'*

What else happened in the town over Christmas 1890? On Christmas Eve geese were plentiful in St. Ives market and sold freely at 9d. per lb. There were two narrow escapes from serious fires in Fore Street. A beam in the flue of Mr. William Faull's house caught fire and a lamp burst at Mr. Adams, fishmonger. A fire occurred in a cellar in Bethesda Place, but fortunately all were extinguished before taking hold.

A strong gale from the NNW drove the Penzance schooner *Secret* ashore on Porthminster beach. The crew were rescued by the lifeboat and after discharging her cargo of coal she was towed off. The Norwegian barque *Julie* bound from Bordeaux to Newport was driven into the Bay. With the help of the St. Ives pilots she was safely moored in the Roads and eventually left with two pilots engaged for the voyage to Newport. On Boxing night the St. Ives Musical Society gave a Christmas Concert in the Public Hall. The room was packed, and despite the provision of additional chairs a great many persons were turned away. Herring catches varied from about 50,000 to 250,000 per day. One day three or four gurries were not sold but thrown over the pierhead. Prices ranged from 1s.6d. to 3s.0d. per hundred.

No births were reported, but Mr. Peter Veal, 86, died at the Meadow; Frances, wife of Mr. Charles Leddra, 74, died at Bellair Terrace, and Mary, daughter of Mr. Richard Edwards, aged 16 months at Victoria Place. Mr. Humphrey Ninnes Quick and Miss Caroline Murrish were married at the Parish Church. One major difference between then and now is no doubt the number of visitors who now come to St. Ives for Christmas. From May to November the *Summary* published a list of visitors to the town — their names and where they came from, and the hotel or lodging where they were staying. Visitors were asked to leave their names at the office of the paper as soon as possible after their arrival and lodging house keepers '. . . *will advance their interests by sending to the publisher the names and addresses of visitors occupying their apartments . . .'* At the height of the season in August, the list occupied nearly two columns, dwindling through September and October until the last few names in the issue for November 1st which included two painters, Mr. Titcomb at 6, The Terrace and Mr. Bosch Reitz at number 7. There was no reference to any visitors over the Christmas period. Any who were in the town were probably staying with relatives or at Tregenna Castle and not as now in self-catering apartments.

As a matter of interest, but nothing to do with Christmas, Mrs. Pearson's residence at 6 The Terrace seemed to be popular as a lodging for artists while they were working in St. Ives. The previous year Mr. E.W. Blomefield and the two Griers, Louis and Wyly, stayed there for the summer season. In 1890 Mr. Titcomb arrived there in June and was still there at the end of October. He was joined by relatives for six weeks in the summer, and in October he attended the funeral of one of his models, Capt. Dick Harry. Capt. Dick was the central figure in the Academy picture 'Primitive Methodists at prayer' and had sat for another picture by Mr. Titcomb only a few days before his death.

Those artists no doubt knew enough about St. Ives not to make the same mistake as the Japanese artist who, arriving on a Sunday in September/October, set up his easel at Chy-an-Chy, close by the harbour and started painting. He had a lively half hour with a number of children who threw missiles at him and threatened to tell the policeman if he didn't clear out. As the *Summary* succinctly put it 'He skedaddled'. I wonder if, like the Pola Negri film unit who suffered verbal missiles 39 years later, he skedaddled over to Newlyn to finish his painting!

Things have changed in many ways since those far-off days, but in the end Christmas is what you make it. Why not think about making it a bit different this year? Get the piano tuned, and dig out the News Chronicle Song Book from the attic. When the Chapel choir appear outside your door go out and join them in a chorus or two of 'Hellesveor,' then ask them in for a glass of hot ginger wine and a mince pie. Better still, instead of sitting round the fire watching the recorded fictional experiences of James Bond, borrow a cassette recorder and record on tape your own real life experiences, memories of your family and St. Ives as it was and is. In the years to come your great-grandchildren and their great-grandchildren will bless you, and in a hundred years when one of them writes about the old days, the Christmas of 2003 could stand out as the one that was a bit different, but rather special.